*Wilfried Müller*

# 111 MORE PORSCHE STORIES THAT YOU SHOULD KNOW

emons:

CONTENTS


MICKEY MOUSE & COFFEE TRAIN | 8

1___ Porsche 356 America Roadster
*The aluminium ancestor* | 10

2___ Porsche 356 B 1600 GS Carrera GTL Abarth Coupé
*Who built the GTL?* | 12

3___ Porsche 530
*The first four-seater, almost* | 16

4___ Porsche 645 Spyder
*One radical Mickey Mouse* | 18

5___ Porsche 904/8 "Kangaroo"
*The wild marsupial* | 20

6___ Porsche 911 2.4 S Tour de France Automobile
*Lightweight 911, heavyweight task* | 22

7___ Porsche 917-053 Magnesium Chassis
*One race, one win* | 26

8___ Porsche 917 Short Tail for the Road
*Make way for the Conte* | 28

9___ Porsche 924 Carrera GT
*The wild cousin* | 32

10___ Porsche 944 Turbo Cup
*Leopard spots and hieroglyphs* | 34

11___ Allgaier P 312
*'Simple, robust, rugged, safe in the tropics!'* | 36

12___ Audi? Opel? Volkswagen?
*Porsche undercover* | 38

ASPHALT & DUST | 42

13___ Weissach test site
*Where the master mechanic spun out* | 44

14___ Targa Florio 1961
*The fastest – until three kilometres from the finish* | 46

15___ London–Sydney Marathon 1968
*A business trip* | 48

16___ Ghost RSR at Le Mans, 1975
*Grid-sneaker, black-flagged* | 50

17___ Monte Carlo Rally 1978
*The win that came out of the blue* | 52

18___ Safari Rally 1978
*Not your typical Easter stroll* | 56

19___ Le Mans 1983
*Engine wrecked, race won* | 58

20___ Le Mans 1988
*Well driven, lost by a whisker* | 60

21___ Le Mans 2017
*Going out with a bang* | 62

SUPER LIGHT & LONG-TAIL | 64

22___ Porsche 356 Super Light
*46 hp, seven men, and a class win* | 66

23___ Porsche 550 Prototype
*A message from reckless days* | 68

24___ Porsche 718 W-RS Spyder
*Forever young* | 70

25___ Porsche 906 Carrera 6
*Fast beauty* | 72

26___ Porsche 907
*270 kph on the Salzburg Autobahn* | 76

27___ Porsche 908/02 Spyder
*The first world champion* | 78

28___ Porsche 935
*Read the rules, win the race* | 82

29___ Porsche 936 Spyder
*Bullseye at first shot* | 86

30___ Porsche 961
*Treading a fine line* | 88

31___ Porsche 962 IMSA
*Born for the USA* | 92

32___ Porsche 911 Turbo S Le Mans GT
*A new start with GT* | 94

33___ Porsche 962 Dauer LM GT
*A slight problem with the '4'* | 96

34___ Porsche 919 Hybrid Evo
*Thunderous swansong* | 98

RACERS & GENTLEMEN | 100

35___ Stefan Bellof
*Speed and laughter* | 102

36___ Timo Bernhard
*'Pretty fast'* | 104

37___ Mark Donohue
*'Captain Nice' and the turbo revolution* | 106

38___ Paul Frère
*A speedy scribe* | 108

39___ Dan Gurney
*Racing history with a difference* | 110

40___ Leo Kinnunen
*Words are silver, action is gold* | 112

41___ Gijs van Lennep
*Turning passion into history* | 116

42___ Jochen Mass
*Steely determination* | 118

43___ Jackie Oliver
*'Close your eyes and hope for the best!'* | 120

44___ Brian Redman
*Triumph and near-tragedy* | 122

45___ Pedro Rodríguez
*Mexican revelation* | 124

46___ Björn Waldegård
*Sensitive antennae* | 126

VISIONS & WIND TUNNELS | 128

47___ 914/6 Count von Görtz
*Exceptional aristocrat* | 130

48___ Porsche 916 Brutus
*Hefty power, hefty price* | 132

49___ World record Porsche 924
*Good for 280 kph – and never run* | 134

50___ Porsche 924 Targa Concepts
*Open-air varieties* | 136

51___ 935/78 Moby Dick 2
*A model athlete* | 138

52___ Porsche 928 S4
*Racetrack and horse trailer* | 140

53___ Porsche 928 S4 Cabriolet Prototype H21
*Roaring and roofless* | 142

54___ Porsche Indy P6B
*Outmanoeuvred* | 144

55___ Porsche 959 Aerodynamics Study C29
*Lofty artefact* | 148

56___ Porsche LMP 2000
*Hidden treasure* | 152

57___ Porsche Cayenne S Jagdwagen
*Hunting Porsche-style* | 154

58___ Porsche Boxster Bergspyder
*Return to adventure* | 156

CARS & A CREST | 158

59___ Porsche 356
*The first one from Stuttgart* | 160

60___ Porsche 356 A 1500 GS Carrera
*How 'Carrera' hit the road* | 164

61___ The Porsche Crest
*It all started with Dr Domnick* | 168

62___ Porsche 356 C 1600 SC Police Cabriolet
*Open-air from five degrees* | 170

63___ Porsche 904 Carrera GTS
*Racing beauty* | 174

64___ 911 Targa
*Money saved, legend born* | 178

65___ Porsche 917-001
*A passion for 001* | 182

66___ Porsche 911 GT2
*Wild Thing!* | 184

67___ Porsche Boxster Spyder
*'More smiles per gallon'* | 188

68___ Porsche Tractor
*Not your usual Porsche* | 190

WORDS & PLACES | 192

69___ Porsche Design
*Superyacht, grand piano, tobacco pipe* | 194

70___ Porsche Museum, Zuffenhausen
*A journey back in time* | 196

71___ Air-Cooled
*Cool to the core* | 200

72___ Clubsport
*Everyday racers* | 202

73___ Porsche Dual-Clutch Gearbox
*A belated triumph* | 204

74___ The Home of Motor Racing
*Made in Flacht* | 206

75___ Porsche Spyder
*Spyder engine? 911 GT1 98 Spyder?* | 208

76___ RS & RSR
*RennSportRennwagen* | 212

77___ The Schüttgut
*Home* | 214

78___ The Fuchs Rim
*Aluminium cult* | 216

79___ Vintage Porsches
*Treasures on wheels* | 218

PIT LANE & EXECUTIVE FLOOR | 220

80___ Bernhard Blank and Rupprecht von Senger
*Swiss courage* | 222

81___ Fritz Enzinger
*Friendly face of success* | 224

82___ Richard von Frankenberg
*Schreckenstein, the all-rounder* | 226

83___ Maximilian Edwin Hoffman
*Nothing by halves* | 228

84___ Roland Kussmaul
*Master of all trades* | 230

85___ Hubert Mimler
*Fastest of all taxi drivers* | 232

86___ Karl Rabe
*Beetle, Gmünd and 356* | 234

87___ Franz Xaver Reimspieß
*Beetle engine and Porsche crest* | 236

88___ Valentin Schäffer
*'I'm thinking of 1,000 hp'* | 238

89___ Peter Werner Schutz
*Lengthened the lifeline* | 240

90___ Alwin Springer
*'To see a bit of the world'* | 242

HELLO & GOODBYE | 244

91___ Rally to the Midnight Sun, 1950
*First factory mission* | 246

92___ Liège–Rome–Liège, 1952
*Knockout in the fog* | 250

93___ 12 Hours of Sebring, 1960
*A nice vacation* | 252

94___ Formula Two at Monaco, 1959
*Porsche's first single-seater* | 254

95___ Nürburgring 1000 km, 1967
*A first home win, a brief flourish* | 258

96___ Inspection of the 917, 1969
*Racing car ready, parking available* | 260

97___ Porsche 917 Leaves the USA, 1975
*Farewell with 1,230 hp* | 262

98___ Downforce vs Top Speed at Le Mans
*The end of a dogma* | 264

99___ China's First Permanent Racetrack
*Premiere at Zhuhai* | 266

AIR & WATER | 268

100___ Generation 1: the First Porsche 911
*S presses ahead* | 270

101___ Generation 2: Porsche 911, G series
*As you like it* | 274

102___ Generation 3: Porsche 911, Type 964
*'We'll make a 4WD 911'* | 278

103___ Generation 4: Porsche 911, Type 993
*Finale furioso* | 282

104___ Generation 5: Porsche 911, Type 996
*Watershed model* | 284

105___ Generation 6: Porsche 911, Type 997
*Don't overdo it!* | 286

106___ Generation 7: Porsche 911, Type 991
*Records, records* | 288

107___ Generation 8: Porsche 911, Type 992
*A clever beast* | 290

WATTS & PUNCH | 294

108___ Electric Pioneer
*Magical energy* | 296

109___ Mission E
*Simply electifying* | 298

110___ Porsche 99X Electric
*High voltage* | 300

111___ Porsche Taycan
*Racing to the future* | 302

# A very warm welcome

to *111 More Porsche Stories*. In volume two of my little book, let's dive even deeper into the characteristic, the unexpected, the spectacular and the amusing that make the fascination of the world's most famous sports car manufacturer.

These are tales of captivating sports cars, from the spartan America Roadster to the e-revolution that Porsche calls Taycan. I share stories of racing cars, such as the highly unconventional Mickey Mouse, the aluminium GT hand-built in Italy, and world champion descendants of the 911. Of exotic cars that never rolled into a garage or onto a starting grid. Come along on automobile adventures from London to Sydney, from Nairobi to northern Sweden, and discover the words and places tied up in myths and dreams. Finally, meet some of the characters who worked behind the wheel, at the drawing board, at a desk or crossed the Sahara at high speed to help give the Porsche name its incomparable aura.

I hope to surprise you with some of these stories and to provide many hours of pleasure. So fasten your seat-belts for the second leg of our journey through the world of Porsche, and enjoy 111 more stops along the way.

Wilfried Müller
Leigh, New Zealand

A Mickey Mouse that really took off, a “coffee train” tractor promoted by a world champion, and an America Roadster like this one. Porsche has created many exotic vehicles over the years.

# MICKEY MOUSE & COFFEE TRAIN

16 10 51

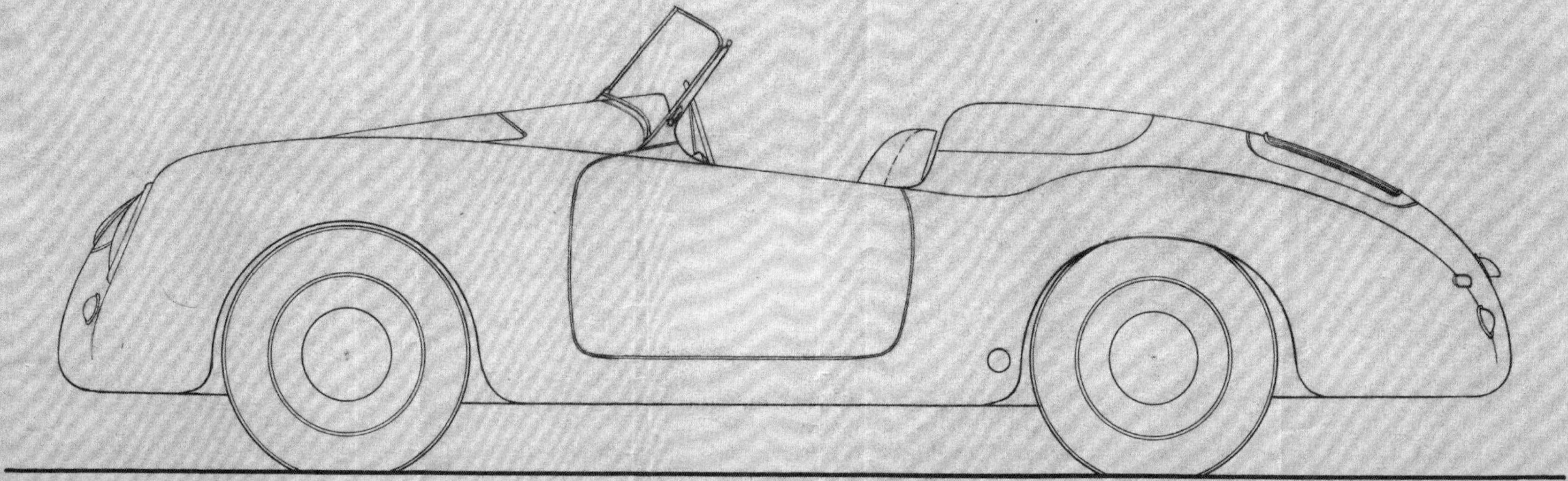

Original der Firma Erich Heuer,
eingegangen mit Brief v. 16.10.51.

Porsche Sport Roadster

000.00.325

16.10.51

# 1__ Porsche 356 America Roadster

*The aluminium ancestor*

'Type 356 Type 540 Racing Roadster for the USA' – these are the words on the cover of the slightly yellowing file in the Porsche company archives. 'America Roadster' is the common name used today for this exotic ancestor of the Speedster. On January 23, 1952, Max E. Hoffman wrote a letter from his address in Park Avenue, New York City, to Ferry Porsche, sending his order no. 5072 as an attachment. It was for '6 aluminium sports roadsters'. Hoffman was one of the biggest importers of exclusive European automobiles to the USA, and knew all too well the importance of the motto: 'Win on Sunday, sell on Monday.' Clearly, he needed a Porsche fit for racing. He also had a very clear idea of how to achieve this: at least 65 hp, easily removable bumpers, comfortable seats, a windscreen that could be replaced by a small Plexiglas shield, large brake drums, removable safety belts, and centre-lock wheels. He specified all of this in his letter.

The body manufacturer Erich Heuer had already presented Porsche with a design for a 'sports roadster' in October 1951 and was now commissioned to construct this minimal two-seater from sheet aluminium. Between the spring of 1952 and the winter of 1953, Heuer made 16 lightweight 356s and one of steel: with and without softtops, with hollow, unclad doors, side windows to slot in instead of wind down, removable windscreen and bumpers. In July 1952, Porsche disclosed the weight of the No. 4 Roadster at 689 kilos, of which some 100 kilos could be shed for a racing weekend. With a 1.5-litre "super" engine generating 70 hp, this lightweight could sprint to 100 kph in just under ten seconds and reach a top speed of over 170 kph.

But it was also expensive, costing twice as much as its English competitors at around 4,500 USD. Production stopped after this mini-series, Heuer was spent. On the West Coast, John von Neumann simply cut the roof off a steel-body 356 Coupé. Yes, this was the beginning of what was to become the successful model with the magical name 'Speedster'.

__ This is what the America Roadster actually looked like, in this case, a rather luxurious version. For racing, it had no roof, bumpers, windscreen or other superfluous accessories.

# 2 Porsche 356 B 1600 GS Carrera GTL Abarth Coupé

*Who built the GTL?*

This is one of those rare Porsches that was styled in Italy, and the only one that was made there. An untamed, elegant GT racing car based on the 356 B that left an indelible impression: winner in its class at the Targa Florio in 1960 and 1961, and the best 1.6-litre at Le Mans in 1960, 1961 and 1962.

The secret of its success was in the air: on March 23, 1960, Porsche put a Carrera GTL into a wind tunnel. The result was 18.4 per cent less drag and a frontal area 8.3 per cent smaller than the conventional Carrera GT. With its 1.6-litre Carrera engine and 115 to 135 hp, the GTL hit speeds over 200 kph. But who really put this Porsche on the road? It's a matter of some speculation. The Porsche archives in Zuffenhausen provide some clues. On November 11, 1959, Porsche placed an order for '20 G.T. Coupé light-metal bodyworks' with an old friend, Carlo Abarth. The racing car maker from Turin promised to deliver them by January 8, 1960. In November, the chassis made their way from Zuffenhausen to Turin. There, at Abarth's behest, they were dispatched to the renowned aluminium shaper Rocco Motto and the sports car maker Siata, as a report by Porsche man Klaus Steinmetz, dated September 19, 1960, shows: 'In the course of the morning, Mr Motto, owner of the workshop where the bodywork for the GTLs is being produced, joined us [...]. From [...] Siata, where our cars will be painted and assembled, came the managing director [...]'. There were 17 GTLs according to Steinmetz. The files cast no light on the origin of the other three.

The delivery from Turin left the Stuttgart crowd speechless. Steinmetz noted the following about an early GTL: 'Wheel guard leaky, headlights defective after the first drive in rain; assembly of seats [...] unacceptable; [...]; roof brace directly over the driver's head, winding-lever of right-hand window falls off; underside of car not painted and rusty in places, water leaks in through the doors [...].' Porsche mechanics worked for up to 150 additional hours to get a GTL ready for sale. But who cares about trivial details if you win your class at Le Mans?

A 356 B 1600 GS Carrera GTL Abarth at the Nürburgring in 1962. Porsche supplied the chassis, Franco Scaglione designed the bodywork. Rocco Motto made 17 cars, Viarenzo & Filliponi probably three.

PORSCHE
Reifenlager
Continental Reifen
1,2 T
29
29
OF JR 1

ontinental-Reifen
ontinental-Re
72

Italian bodywork, Swabian inner workings: the Porsche 356 B 1600 GS Carrera GTL Abarth. Herbert Linge drives the car in an airfield race, 1963.

# 3_ Porsche 530

*The first four-seater, almost*

This was Porsche's first attempt to enable a family of four to travel at sports-car speeds. Based on the 356, Type 530 was created in 1951–52 in a coupé and a cabriolet version. The vehicle was powered by the tried-and-tested 60 horsepower, 1.5-litre, four-cylinder, pushrod engine, mounted, of course, behind the rear axle.

Astonishingly, the company's internal notes on the 'sports coupé' and the cabriolet record an identical weight of 918 kg for both cars, which certainly suggests sporty performance. Top speed was reached at 155 kph. To create legroom in the back, the wheelbase was increased by 30 centimetres to 2.40 metres. The elongated roofline swept in a convex-concave shape to the engine lid and the rear. This created more headroom for the passengers in the back. Larger doors allowed reasonably elegant entry to the second row of seating. However, as the passengers in the back sat between the wheel housings, the space available to them was somewhat restricted. The small luggage compartment under the front lid made it advisable to pack lightly or send a suitcase ahead by rail. The folding softtop with a lining offered additional comfort for the cabriolet passengers, and the side windows at the rear could be wound down – a bona fide cabriolet for four, from Porsche, back in 1952.

However, as the literature suggests, Ferry Porsche insisted on the rear-sloping roofline that was a characteristic trademark of his sports cars, and the long wheelbase also irked the company patriarch. It also seemed daring for a young sports car manufacturer to venture into the market segment of well-established sedan manufacturers. What's more, the small factory with some 260 employees, as well as the bodywork shops of Reutter and Heuer with 300 workers, were already stretched to breaking point with the production of the successful 356 model.

— This coupé with an extended wheelbase was intended to carry four passengers. Ferry Porsche rejected the idea. He insisted on the roofline sloping to the rear and the agility of the original 356.

# 4_ Porsche 645 Spyder

*One radical Mickey Mouse*

A datasheet from the racing development department in Zuffenhausen noted the following on the short and spectacular life of the 645 Spyder in 1956: 'In operation 22.7.1956 to 16.9.1956. Race at Solitude on 22.7.56, driver: v. Frankenberg, 14th place. 8.56 Nürburgring, practice only … 16.9.56 Avus, Berlin, driver: v. Frankenberg, vehicle took off, crashed in the paddock and burned out.'

The 645 was conceived in late 1954 by the engineer Egon Forstner as a successor to the 550. To achieve low drag, a diminutive Spyder emerged, its dimensions no more than 1.42 metres wide and 90 centimetres high. The track beneath the close-fitting magnesium bodywork measured 1.19 metres at the front and 1.15 metres at the rear. Total length: 377 centimetres. The rear wheels were partly covered; the front end 'boldly curving' as the datasheet states. Instead of an air intake for the oil radiator, a system of pipes beneath the front bonnet would keep the lubricant at a healthy temperature. The 110 hp, 1.5-litre engine received air through a slit directed towards the rear, and aided by decent aerodynamics, powered the 645 to a little over 260 kph. With a wheelbase of 1.94 metres and centrally placed fuel tanks, the Spyder was agile, and the wonderful double-wishbone rear axle proved far superior to its longitudinal link counterpart at the front. This led to nasty understeer, followed by the rear end abruptly trying to overtake the car. All in all, in the opinion of the works driver Richard von Frankenberg, when braking and cornering, the 645 handled like a scurrying mouse – this was the "Mickey Mouse."

On September 16, 1956, von Frankenberg tackled the Berlin Grand Prix at the wheel of the mouse. On lap three, the 645 skidded out of the banked north curve at high speed, became airborne and crashed in the paddock. Von Frankenberg was thrown from the cockpit shortly after take-off and spent the next five weeks in hospital. The 645 was history, but it taught the racing department a few lessons for the 550A, the successor that triumphed instead of scurrying.

__ September 16, 1956: Richard von Frankenberg in the 645 hurtling around the banked north curve of the Avus racetrack in Berlin. The active career of the Mickey Mouse is about to come to an end.

9
9

# 5_ Porsche 904/8 'Kangaroo'

*The wild marsupial*

The 901 in 1963, the 904 Carrera GTS in 1964: Ferdinand Alexander Porsche produced two epoch-making sports car designs in quick succession. And then this one: the 904/8 Bergspyder in 1965. It resembled one of those dune buggies that had been zipping around Californian beaches since 1963: roofless, plastic bodywork with minimal overhangs and a small windshield in front of the driver. Weighing 520 kilograms, the Spyder was 120 kilos lighter than the 904 Coupé. It also had plenty of grunt: Porsche's Type 771, a 2-litre, eight-cylinder engine generating 260 hp at 8,800 revs, sat in front of the rear axle. From a standing start, the 904/8 reached 100 kph in just under three seconds and achieved a top speed of 260 kph.

This lightweight was intended for serpentine rampages like those experienced at the Targa Florio and the European championship hill climbs, which explains its minimalistic appearance. As a faithful adherent of the motto that form follows function, F. A. Porsche had logically discarded most things. Colin Davis and Gerhard Mitter accomplished a brilliant debut for the Spyder with second place at the Targa Florio on May 9, 1965. This was a fantastic achievement given that Porsche's international stars Jo Bonnier and Graham Hill had flatly refused to compete in the Spyder in Sicily after their first taste at the wheel. Without a roof, the 904 chassis proved too soft, and after shedding 120 kilos it proved almost impossible to find a decent suspension setup. Soon, the Spyder was known simply as 'the Kangaroo'. In the European Hillclimb Championship it yielded a solitary win for Gerhard Mitter, but astonishingly he was able to win at the Norisring and the Solitude racetracks. Even before the European hill climb season ended, Porsche replaced the marsupial after only eight starts with the progressive Ollon Villars Spyder. In 1966, private drivers competed at Daytona, Palm Beach and Sebring as well as in the Bahamas Cup with this idiosyncratic racing car, of which only five examples were produced in Zuffenhausen.

___ It looked like a dune buggy and went like the devil. The 904/8 'Kangaroo', here with Graham Hill practicing the 1965 Targa Florio. The Briton found the handling atrocious and refused to race the car.

# 6_ Porsche 911 2.4 S Tour de France Automobile

*Lightweight 911, heavyweight task*

Where rallying was concerned, the repair department at Porsche artfully prepared the machinery in the 1960s and 1970s. On June 10, 1970, repair order no. 71309400 wafted into the intray. It related to the 911, 'registration plate S-U 9370, registered 19.3.1970, mileage 15,598 km, chassis no. 911 030 1127, engine no. 630 1557.' The task was to make this 911 fit for the Tour de France Automobile in September – a 4,600-kilometre loop around the beautiful country, with high-speed side trips to nine racetracks and ten hill climbs. The car was to be driven by the previous year's winner, Gérard Larrousse. The technicians' instructions included the following: 'Take car, engine, gearbox apart, instal 40% locking diff, change gear ratios... instal reworked engine...' Point 7 instructed: 'make the vehicle as light as possible.'

Lightweight! No one did this better than the Zuffenhausen crew. First, they threw out all non-essentials: from hood locks to the cover of the glove compartment. Everything that had to stay was made lighter. The front wings and bumpers, hood, doors, side and rear windows were plastic, the bodywork consisted mainly of sparsely painted, thin sheet metal. To shed weight, everything without a load-bearing function was cut out or drilled, right down to the handle of the fuel-tank cap. The team did a thorough job, after all, they were Swabians, and what's more, Larrousse had promised a bottle of champagne for every cast-off kilo.

Ultimately, this Porsche tipped the scales at 789 kilos (with 10 litres of fuel in the tank, Larrousse recalls). The engine was enlarged by 200 cc to 2,396 cc, and produced 250 hp at 8,000 revs with titanium pistons and two triple carburettors. The first four gears were short, while the fifth allowed a top speed of 245 kph. Its toughest rivals were two Matra MS 650 space-frame racing cars, which presumably got permission to compete for patriotic reasons. Larrousse and his co-driver Maurice Gélin put in a breathtaking performance to cross the line in Nice in third place with their production-based Nine-Eleven behind the two French prototypes.

— The lightest 911 that ever took to the road was this 911 S 2.4 in 1970. 789 kilograms, painted in the psychedelic style of the day. With 250 hp, it maxed out at 245 kph.

DUNLOP
BOSCH
Shell
CIBIE
MARTINI
LARROUSSE
SHELL

An amazing sight for racing fans: Gérard Larrousse's beautiful Porsche 911 S 2.4 at scrutineering for the 1970 Tour de France Automobile.

GELIN
LARROUSSE
139
SHELL

# 7_ Porsche 917-053 Magnesium Chassis

*One race, one win*

Here comes a true exotic! Porsche had already won the world championship and Le Mans in 1970 with the 917. In their relentless quest for further fractions of seconds and pushing the limits of lightweight construction, the decision was made in December to make the space frame from magnesium instead of aluminium.

No sooner said than welded. In spring 1971, the magnesium chassis 917-051 began its 1,000-kilometre test at Weissach, including two stretches of brutally rough road. The sport's regulations required a minimum weight of 800 kilos. 051 weighed just 722.6 kilos, crumbled swiftly during testing and was scrapped. 917-052 was reinforced, and survived the torturous tests without any problems. It proved very fast during the pretests at Le Mans, underwent more testing at Weissach and was scrapped in September. The third and last magnesium chassis, 917-053, was produced for the race. The scales registered 766 kilos for the short-tail racer, which is why the engine oil tank was generously sized at 55 litres. For the race, Porsche entrusted this unique 917 to the Dutch driver Gijs van Lennep and the Austrian Helmut Marko. The 12-cylinder, 4.9-litre engine produced around 600 hp and propelled the 917 to 360 kph. As expected, the more streamlined long-tail 917s turned faster lap times. The magnesium 917 started the marathon from fifth on the grid. It pitted twice when the alternator belt came off but otherwise raced on without any problems. In fact, it raced so well that Lennep and Marko found themselves in the lead after the 13th hour. Three hours from the finish, the mechanics discovered cracks in the front brake discs. Replace them or carry on? 'Carry on!' the drivers cried. On the orders of team management, they increased their lap times by four to five seconds, but nevertheless, the mission remained risky. Lennep and Marko managed to nurse the car over the line in first place and set a distance record that remained unbroken for 39 years. The only magnesium 917 in the world now lives in the Porsche Museum in Zuffenhausen.

__ The magnesium 917 on the way to victory at Le Mans in 1971. Not even the drivers knew what material the frame was made from.

DUNLOP DUNLOP
22
MARTINI
RACING-TEAM
PORSCHE

# 8__ Porsche 917 Short-Tail for the Road

*Make way for the Conte*

Fencing, horses, motorboat racing: Conte (Count) Metello Rossi di Montelera (1903–1972) was a sportsman. He also sat on a small fortune, thanks to his Martini & Rossi company that produced vermouth and prosecco for connoisseurs around the globe. In 1958, the Conte founded the Martini International Club to promote sports and culture. His sons Gregorio and Vittorio kept their father's pet project going, founding Martini Racing in 1970 and devoting themselves with a passion to Porsche motor racing.

Gregorio (1936–2003), in particular, enjoyed the atmosphere in the Porsche pits, undertaking his sponsorship in a generous and nonchalant manner. In 1970, when the Porsche designers came up with the idea of entering the long-tail 917 of the Martini Racing Team as a 'hippie car' flying minuscule Martini stickers, Gregorio gave a casual nod – as he did a year later for the 917/20 'pig'. Martini and Porsche were the very best of friends, and the 917, 936 and Carrera RSR all chalked up victories in the red-and-blue-striped design. In November 1974, Conte Gregorio took delivery of the then one and only 917 fit for road use from Weissach, as a souvenir of this partnership: with a 5-litre V12 and probably just less than 600 hp for a little over 800 kilos. The approval for road use by the authorities turned out to be an obstacle course, however. Gregorio lived in Paris, and the French demanded a crash test – which was impossible. The Italians simply said: 'no, Grazie.' But in Alabama, they gave the nobleman and his Porsche beast the thumbs-up: 'Okay, you can have your registration plate. Under one condition: here in Alabama you don't drive a single metre with the 917.'

For the trip from Weissach to Paris, Porsche had informed the Conte: '130 kph equals about 4,000 revs in second gear.' At the French border – as the story is now told at Porsche – a gendarme was waiting for Rossi and told him: 'That's a wonderful car. Now give it some throttle. Just this once, there is no speed limit for you here.'

So, le bon vieux temps! Gregorio's son Manfredo took over the 917 with chassis number 030 and still takes it on occasional outings at Goodwood or Laguna Seca.

__ Conte Rossi's short-tail 917 added a touch of racing to his daily aristocratic rounds. The Conte collected the 917 in 1974, and now his son occasionally takes the Porsche for a spin.

DUNLOP
DUNLOP

___ Have another look and enjoy: Count Gregorio Rossi di Montelara picked up 917-030 from Weissach on 8 November, 1974. And off he was on his way to Paris...

# 9__ Porsche 924 Carrera GT

*The wild cousin*

A 924 for around 60,000 Deutschmarks! More expensive than a 911 SC or a Targa. That's the 924 Carrera GT. Porsche made this transaxle sports car in 1980 as a homologation special for competing on racetracks and in rallies. Above all, it was intended to polish up the rather sedate image of the 924 'family-sport hatchback' (as Porsche advertising put it) that had been on sale since spring 1976. With a water-cooled front engine from Audi, 125 hp (in the USA and Japan it was more like 100) and easy handling thanks to its transaxle construction, the 924 lacked what it took to create the myth of a tough sports machine or to give goosebumps like the 911.

The 924 Carrera GT did both: thanks to an output of 210 hp from a 1,984 cc engine with turbocharger and intercooler, forged pistons, sharper camshafts and higher compression. At 106 hp, the power output per litre marked a record for road-legal automobiles. Thin glass and light sheet metal saved weight. The front bonnet and doors were made of aluminium, the front spoiler, the wide wings and the scoop on the bonnet were of fibre-reinforced plastic. Sports suspension, wide tyres on Fuchs wheels and the brakes taken from the 3.3-litre 911 Turbo made for precise handling and impressive deceleration. With sports seats, a small leather steering wheel and upholstery in red-and-black pinstripes, the interior looked sporty and chic. The wildest 924 for the road weighed 1,180 kilos, managed zero to 100 kph in 6.9 seconds, and was good for a top speed of 240 kilometres per hour.

Weissach produced 406 cars – just a few more than were necessary for sports homologation. Motor journals raved about the powerful turbo thrust at 4,500 revs, waxed lyrical about having to grab the steering wheel firmly and reported crazy cornering speeds. In February 1981, half a year after the start of production, every 924 Carrera GT had been sold. Before long, racing and rally versions based on this sports car with up to 375 hp reaped a rich harvest of trophies.

__ On the right, the basic road model, on the left its wild Le Mans cousin. Even the road version of the 924 Carrera GT, weighing only 1,180 kilos, was extremely fast.

4
BILSTEIN
SCHMITTHELM
DUNLOP
Turbolader
BOSCH
DUNLOP
Shell

# 10_ Porsche 944 Turbo Cup

*Leopard spots and hieroglyphs*

In 1986, Porsche ran its own one-make cup series for the first time. Amateurs and professionals in their 220 hp Porsche 944 Turbo Cup racers went head-to-head for prize money, points and prestige in front of big crowds at national racetracks. The near-standard racing cars were identical down to the very last screw, consumed standardised fuel in their 2.5-litre inline engines, and rolled to the start on control tyres and with sealed ECUs. Three-way catalytic converters that didn't cost horsepower, and ABS adapted for racing were new and cutting-edge technical solutions.

For 1987, Porsche upped the ante. The engine performance increased to 250 hp. The sprint from zero to 100 kph took 6.3 seconds, and if the straight was long enough, the 944 Turbo Cup reached 260 kilometres per hour. The idea of a one-make cup proved a success. Of the ten events, five were contested in Germany, with five more run in other European countries. Two 944 Turbos, with a special livery conceived and executed by the German artist Manfred Herbst, were reserved for prominent guest drivers. The spotted pattern, according to the literature, represented the speed of the leopard. The punched tape – a common storage medium for computers back then – symbolised the blessings of modern technology. The painted hieroglyphs denoted a message from the depths of history, sending salutations to the 'gods of the race', for example an appeal from the drivers for 'protection in the race' (according to the artist's website) and to grant victory in the forthcoming clash.

Porsche can look back on the history of their one-make cups as a resounding success. In 1990, the 911 replaced the 944 Turbo as the cup racer. In 2020, 21 Porsche one-make cups, challenges and trophies were planned for drivers and teams at all levels of professionalism and all around the world. Again and again, top racing drivers, whose names now grace the winners' list at Le Mans, have emerged from this huge talent pool.

— Leopard spots, punched tape and hieroglyphs – the design of this 944 Turbo racing car from 1987 effortlessly bridges themes and millennia.

BLAUPUNKT
BLAUPUNKT
DUNLOP
Shell
BLAU
1
Turbo Cup
PAGID
RECARO

# 11_Allgaier P 312

*"Simple, robust, rugged, safe in the tropics!"*

This was the promise made in Portuguese in the headline of a Brazilian brochure for a plantation tractor that was also known as the 'coffee train'. The brochure drew particular attention to the 30 hp air-cooled, petrol-run Porsche engine. Yes, petrol – because diesel vapours wreak havoc on the sensitive aroma of coffee beans. The P 312, with an extra-narrow track and a specially developed 'Ackerwolf' cultivator, was designed to prepare the soil and remove weeds between the rows of coffee plants in the vast plantations of South America. Among its other qualities, the text praises its light weight of just 1,275 kilograms as a particular advantage on sensitive soils. Finally, the brochure mentions the 'elegant exterior' as another attractive feature of the tractor.

The 'coffee train' is without doubt the most streamlined Allgaier Porsche tractor ever made. The cladding on the wheels even drew comparisons with Le Mans sports cars. However, the curvaceous shape of the metal bodywork was not intended for ventures at record-breaking velocities, but rather to reduce damage to the vulnerable coffee bushes. With a working speed of 2.6 kph, the P 312 may well be the slowest Porsche ever to grace this planet.

Allgaier manufactured this exotic machine in Friedrichshafen on Lake Constance. A Brazilian customer expressed interest in an order of 1,000 coffee trains, and freighter ships transported the first 200 orange tractors across the Atlantic to Brazil in 1954. According to reports, the agreed purchase price did not make the return journey across the ocean. The rest of the order remained unfulfilled and no new orders were received, hence production was halted after the first batch. This makes the P 312 a genuine rarity, considering that a total of more than 25,000 'Porsche system' Allgaier tractors were manufactured. It is not clear how many 'coffee trains' have survived. Experts in the field speak of four specimens at most.

The plantation tractor or 'coffee train' at work. At the wheel is the five-time Formula 1 world champion Juan Manuel Fangio, who promoted the slowest Porsche of all time in South America.

# 12_ Audi? Opel? Volkswagen?

*Porsche undercover*

An Opel Manta, a red Audi 100 Coupé, a Volkswagen kombi, an MAN truck ... in the Algerian Sahara in the mid-1970s. Where's Porsche? Though there was no hint on the outside, Porsche was definitely inside three of the four.

The Audi 100 Coupé was one of three vehicles sporting the four rings badge and hiding the complete technology of the imminent Porsche 928 under its skin. The Manta was, in fact, a complete Porsche 924: engine, transaxle, wheels and suspension, the lot. Camouflaged in this way, the Porsches underwent challenging heat tests in the desert between May and September. For every day of testing, some 1,500 kilometres of high-speed driving was on the agenda. The morning journey from the base of the testing crew in the oasis town of El Golea to In Salah accounted for about 800 kilometres. In the afternoon, the return trip from the hotel to Timimoun put a further 720 kilometres on the clock.

The Volkswagen kombi was home-tuned and the pride and joy of head mechanic Ekkehard Kiefer, who had transplanted the 90 hp, 1.6-litre engine of a Porsche 356B Super 90 into the rear and turned the interior with a workbench, cupboards and shelves into the fastest repair shop in the Sahara. This was necessary, as the long, straight tracks easily allowed even a Porsche to run at full throttle for hours at a time, and Kiefer did not want the test drivers to wait around too long for his services. In fact, the testing department rarely set off without the VW. Over its career, this special VW kombi Porsche also spent time north of the Arctic Circle and even made it – aboard a Lockheed Super Constellation – to South Africa.

Although the four-wheel-drive MAN truck that had come from the German army was not powered by a Porsche engine, its links to the sports car manufacturer were close. The truck had belonged to the former Porsche racing driver Paul-Ernst Strähle (1927–2010) and had transported the famous 917/20 'pig' racing car to Le Mans in 1971.

___ The Algerian Sahara, mid-1970s. Members of the testing team take a break. With the exception of the MAN truck, all of the cars in this photograph were powered by Porsche engines.

LEO.
ZA 13

A market square in Algeria in the 1970s. The two Audi coupés are Porsche 928s in disguise, the MAN truck is genuine, the VW kombi hides a Porsche engine.

Safari Rally, 1978. A fast Porsche chase car and the team's plane, which landed on a country road. The works team went looking for challenges all around the world.

# ASPHALT & DUST

# 13_ Weissach Test Site

*Where the master mechanic spun out*

Since the 1960s, every new sports and racing car was taken through its paces on the Weissach test site close to the offices and workshops of the R&D Centre. It all started with the inauguration of the circular skidpad in October 1962. This was followed by the twisty 2.88 kilometres of the "Bergstrecke" (mountain circuit) and the considerably faster 2.53-kilometre Can-Am track in 1968. Whereas some corners were given local names such as 'David's tree', others are anecdotal. The 'Obermeister Kurve' got its moniker from the legendary master mechanic and eventual manager of the entire Weissach site, Herbert Linge. Linge spun off the track spectacularly in a 356 GT a few weeks after the 'mountain circuit' was opened. And the fast, adverse-camber right-hander over a ridge is called the 'Bott chicane' because the former head of development, Helmuth Bott, flatly refused to take the sting out of this hairy bend. Naturally, the racing department set the records. Peter Falk, then head of racing, achieved a record on the circular, 190-metre-diameter skidpad in 1984: 14.4 seconds at the wheel of a short-tail 956, with an average speed of 150.567 kph and 1.858 G of lateral force over the entire lap. It still stands today. On November 9, 1988, the racing engineer Roland Kussmaul turned a record lap of 1:13.28 minutes on the 'mountain circuit' with the March Indy single-seater.

Changes in regulations and corresponding technology, tyres, aerodynamics and weight prove to be obstacles to a well-founded time comparison down the years. Nevertheless, here it is: In July 1970, the record for the Can-Am course, set by Willi Kauhsen in a short-tail 917, stood at 51.5 seconds. In 1986, the stopwatch registered 44.9 seconds for Hans-Joachim Stuck in a 962 C. In October 1990, Italian driver Michele Alboreto managed 41.8 seconds in a 505-kilo Arrows Formula 1 with 700 Porsche horsepower. In spring 2018, works driver Timo Bernhard was clocked at a hell-raising 40.6 seconds in a 919 Hybrid Evo weighing 900 kilos and boasting 1,000+hp – a feat that is unlikely to be matched for years to come.

__ Porsche stories were written on dust and asphalt. Dust was certainly kicked up when these 356 Bs drifted around the skidpad at the opening of the Weissach test track on October 15, 1962.

# 14_ Targa Florio 1961

*The fastest – until three kilometres from the finish*

The last week in April 1961: the 45th Targa Florio runs as the second round of the sports car world championship. Porsche and Ferrari are the favourites in this 720-kilometre race against the clock. The Germans won here in 1959 and 1960. On the latter occasion, Jo Bonnier and Hans Herrmann in a 1.6-litre Porsche 718 RS60 beat Count Berghe von Trips and Phil Hill in a 2.4-litre Ferrari by six minutes. Now, Porsche entered a 718 RS61 with a new 2-litre engine generating 185 hp for a weight of 540 kilos. Stirling Moss and Graham Hill drove a Spyder, Bonnier and Dan Gurney a coupé. Herrmann and Edgar Barth competed in a 718 RS61 Spyder with a 1.6-litre engine. Ferrari pulled two new 246 SPs with 240 hp for 590 kilos out of their hat. These were the first mid-engine racing cars from Maranello: the Commendatore had finally abandoned his philosophy that the ox should be in front of the cart and not behind it. He called on his drivers Berghe von Trips with Olivier Gendebien, and Phil Hill with Richie Ginther. This was a duel for prestige of the highest calibre.

The story of this race through the hills of northern Sicily would be dominated by Stirling Moss and Berghe von Trips. Moss had set a new record during practice in open traffic and was slightly faster than Trips. In the race, Moss turned record laps from the start and was in the lead when he handed the Porsche to Hill, who was caught by Gendebien. Moss, unleashed, took the wheel of the Porsche again for the last 300 kilometres. Gendebien lost time and the lead through an overly cautious stop for refuelling. A furious Trips took over the 246 SP for the last lap over 72 kilometres and turned a record lap in his desperate attempt to catch Moss. He was unaware that Moss's differential had expired 3,000 metres short of the finish line. Moss tried to salvage his victory by leaping out of his car and pushing the 718 RS61 home, but the differential was stuck. Trips and Gendebien won for Ferrari. Zuffenhausen was beaten on this day but was to become the record-holder with eight further triumphs in the years to 1973.

___ Stirling Moss in the 718 RS61 at the Targa Florio in 1961. The British driver in the Swabian racing car held the lead until kilometre 717 of 720 when the differential died.

136
136

# 15 London–Sydney Marathon 1968

*A business trip*

By car from London to Sydney in 1968: England–France–Italy–Yugoslavia–Bulgaria–Turkey–Iran–Afghanistan–Pakistan–India–Australia. 16,700 kilometres, flat-out, except for a short break in Kabul and time to relax on the Indian Ocean aboard SS Chusan while sailing from Bombay to Perth in Western Australia.

There was no doubt about it: Porsche had to be there. Huschke von Hanstein, head of press relations, informed the personnel department: 'The European rally champion Sobieslav Zasada with Marek Wachowski as co-driver, and the Africa specialists Edgar Herrmann and Hans Schuller are taking a business trip with their 911 Ts from November 24 until December 17.' Terry Hunter and John Davenport joined in with a 911 S from Porsche England. The repairs department prepared the cars – with roll bars all-round, underride guard, reinforced chassis and suspension, steel nets, tubes to extend the exhaust in deep water, and four spare wheels on the roof. The cars were also equipped with a jack, an axe, a hand pulley, five warning flares, two cable winches and snow chains. The 2-litre engines produced 160 hp, the gearing allowed a top speed of 200 kph. The clutch could be 'rinsed' with a powder fire extinguisher if it slipped. With the cars weighing 1,400 kilos, head of department, Helmuth Bott, complained that they were 'much too heavy'. The brake lines also caused trouble, which was why Zasada ranked only 13th by the time he reached Bombay. Herrmann was in 27th and Hunter was already on his way home: damaged pistons just out of Kabul after a 23-hour pursuit on gravel tracks.

Navigation was easy: simply aim between the rows of packed spectators. And where there were no crowds, trails of empty soup cans left by the rally crews showed the way. In Australia, the flat-sixes devoured 5 litres of oil per 1,000 kilometres, but the 911s were now the fastest in the race. Alas, it was a little too late: Zasada reached Sydney 4th out of 56 finishers, while Herrmann drove his 911 on five cylinders to arrive in 15th place. Ordeals of this kind were considered normal, even irresistible, in the 1960s.

A 911 T for the rough stuff, with state-of-the-art modifications thanks to the repair department. With 160 hp and short gearing, this 911 was good for speeds up to 200 kph.

# 16_ Ghost RSR at Le Mans 1975

*Grid-sneaker, black-flagged*

Fausto Merello (1940–2014) and Guillermo Ortega (1945–2004) were not only among the fastest drivers in Ecuador in the 1960s and 1970s - they were also among the wealthiest. In 1968, the two friends bought a Ferrari 250 LM and raced it to eighth place at the 24 Hours of Daytona. Merello is recorded as having been the driver of the Italian sports car until 1971. (At a Sotheby's auction in 2013 it fetched a price of 14.3 million USD). The pair turned up at Le Mans for the first time in 1973 and drove a Porsche 908/02 belonging to Ortega to a commendable seventh place. Joined by their compatriot Lothar Ranft, they started a year later in the same Porsche but dropped out after an accident.

Things turned a little hazy in 1975. Ortega shared a 908/02 Spyder with three French drivers supplied by Christian Poirot but failed to qualify. In the meantime, Merello had bought a 911 Carrera RSR, which was to race in the colours of Team Marlboro Ecuador with himself, Fernando Madera and Luis Larrea at the wheel. According to contemporary reports, the car headed to Le Mans with almost no preparation and only achieved 60th place in qualifying. Unfortunately, no more than 55 cars were allowed to compete. But then, just before the start, the four Ferraris campaigned by the North American Racing Team dropped out after a dispute with the Automobile Club de l'Ouest. Amidst the general confusion, Team Marlboro Ecuador promptly stepped into the breach and stealthily put the black 911 Carrera RSR, with starting number nine, into position on the grid.

Merello set off to tackle the 24 Heures after all. However, for our resourceful Ecuadorian, the race only lasted three laps or about fifteen minutes. The black flag came out and he was disqualified. Hence, Le Mans 1975 turned out to be far from a resounding sporting success for Merello & Co., but their appropriation of the grid spot has become a unique and delightful chapter in Le Mans history.

___ The No. 9 car at Le Mans. The sponsorship contract allegedly stipulated that they would only get the money if they started. So that's what the Ecuador team did.

2
9
9
S.E.V.
F MADERA
MARCHAL

# 17_Monte Carlo Rally 1978

*The win that came out of the blue*

Lancia or Fiat would win the 1978 Monte Carlo Rally – there was no question about it. Sandro Munari had driven the all-conquering Lancia Stratos to victory here for three years running. This time, two of the mid-engine, wedge-shaped works cars rolled to the starting line. Four Fiat 131 Abarths also showed up, with rallying virtuosos the likes of Bernard Darniche and Walter Röhrl at the wheel. The two works Renault 5 Alpines with front-wheel drive and 130 hp were deemed to have no chance at all. Just like Jean-Pierre Nicolas and his co-driver Vincent Laverne with their private Porsche 911.

Nicolas, born in Marseille in 1945 and known to his friends as 'Jumbo', had underlined his calibre as a works driver between 1968 and 1974, mastering the difficult rear-engine Alpine A110. Nevertheless, entering in a private 911 seemed bold to the extreme. The 1975 911 Coupé was prepared by the Porsche specialists Jean-Marie and Jacques Alméras with a competitive chassis and suspension. They also implanted an engine from a Carrera RS 3.0, tuned to a conservative 250 hp. Nicolas's old friends at Michelin provided the tyres, which would prove a decisive factor. When the time came for practice, Vincent Laverne found himself snowed-in at an Alpine ski resort. While the works teams recced the route for weeks, Nicolas only managed three days in a Peugeot 104. Depending on who tells the story, he and Laverne either sat in the car together for just one day or not at all.

Then the rally began. Lancia and Fiat were shod with the wrong tyres for cold weather, snow and mud. Munari retired with engine trouble. Out in front were Nicolas and, to everyone's surprise, the R5s. What they had in common were Michelin tyres and engines on the driven axle – at the front of the Renault, at the rear of the Porsche. After racing 470 kilometres against the clock, Nicolas drove his 911 down to Monte Carlo as the overall winner. Second and third places went to the two little Renaults. Nicolas's triumph was the fourth and last for a 911 at the Monte Carlo Rally and, simultaneously, the first Porsche win at a round of the Manufacturer's World Rally Championship.

Nicolas's 911 before the start of the 1978 Monte Carlo Rally. The Alméras brothers had prepared the car superbly. An impeccably driven rally ended with victory number four for a 911 at the 'Monte'.

GITANES
GITANES
GITANES
3
1978
1978
CIBIE
8737 RG 34
PORSCHE ALMERAS

___ Jean-Pierre Nicolas and Vincent Laverne in their private Porsche 911 Carrera RS at the Monte Carlo Rally in 1978. The pair scored a surprise victory against major works teams.

GITANES
3
CIBIE
PORSCHE ALMERAS

# 18_ Safari Rally 1978

*Not your typical Easter stroll*

So many things can happen on a Safari Rally covering some 5,000 kilometres through Eastern Africa! In the night from Maundy Thursday to Good Friday in 1978, after a chase over washboards and through abysmally deep potholes, the front right-hand shock absorber on Vic Preston Junior's 911 SC died. Preston radioed for help, which was waiting at the foot of the Cherangani Hills: the two-man service crew had a fresh suspension strut at the ready, but first had to take out the broken one, which was red hot, with no water in sight to cool it down. No worries! Porsche's man on the spot Roland Kussmaul simply poured 20 litres of petrol over it. It worked. Preston powered on in his 250-horsepower 911.

At 1,180 kilos, the Porsche was a lightweight compared to the Safari vehicles from Datsun, Mercedes and Peugeot. The SC was braced for everything, with a six-millimetre aluminium underride guard, 28 centimetres ground clearance and a sealed engine compartment to ensure that dust could not grind down the piston rings. Well, almost everything: Preston twice changed a half-axle on Easter Sunday and reached the finish in Nairobi in second place, 37 minutes behind the winner.

His team colleague Björn Waldegård had won here in 1977 with a Ford and was in the lead in his 911 at the halfway stage. He lost an hour and his lead when his armoured rear axle broke. A little later, he hit a vulture while driving at high speed. The bird burst through his windscreen and ended up inside the Porsche. The service team was quick to help, but Björn's car was now filled with an impressive aroma of carrion. On the way to Nairobi, a shock absorber broke. Björn replaced it himself, but later the throttle linkage gave up the ghost. Still, the Swede continued through an endless series of mudholes, across rivers and roads that had been swept away by floods, reaching the finish in fourth place. After narrowly missing out on Safari success in 1973 and 1974, victory in Africa once again eluded the Porsche factory squad. The company did not return to East Africa, but would cause a sensation a few years later and many kilometres further north in the Paris–Dakar Rally.

The beautiful 911 SC 3.0 Safari before the start of the 1978 Safari Rally. The works team's last attempt to win this 5,000-kilometre sprint across East Africa ended with second and fourth places.

MARTINI
14
MARTINI PORSCHE
V. PRESTON
J. LYALL
BOSCH
Shell
MARTINI PORSCHE
B. WALDEGAARD
H. THORSZELIUS

# 19_ Le Mans 1983

*Engine wrecked, race won*

The feud for victory at Le Mans in 1983 would go down to the wire between two Porsche 956s. Following a blameless crash and a good deal of technical misfortune, Porsche's superstars Jacky Ickx and Derek Bell were hot on the bumper of the 956 driven by the Americans Hurley Haywood and Al Holbert with the Australian Vern Schuppan.

The pecking order was clear: Ickx and Bell were driving the number one car. But it was also clear that Porsche regarded team orders as unsporting. Consequently, the competition was fierce. Ickx and Bell were catching up fast. The leaders pitted, with Holbert jumping into the driver's seat and taking off without closing the door properly. This was not a problem, as a safety catch prevented it from opening, however, Holbert tried to pull the door shut at more than 300 kph on the straight. At this speed, a hurricane rages above the car. It tore the door open, and then off, hinges and all. Emergency repairs in the pits – first with duct tape, then with a leather belt – brought moderate success. At high speed, the door opened slightly and disturbed the airflow to the water-cooler in the wing. Holbert radioed in that the water temperature had reached 110° Celsius. With 20 minutes left on the clock, it had risen even further. Ickx and Bell pulled out all stops. With his brakes failing, Bell set two lap records in the final hour.

The pit crew serving Haywood, Holbert and Schuppan had no choice: if they pulled in the ailing 956, victory would be lost. Out on the track, the engine was expiring. Holbert declutched, engaged the clutch again … and the six-cylinder sputtered back to life. The pit crew then saw him coming through the last chicane. From his cockpit, Bell now spotted the 956 a stone's throw ahead of him. White smoke billowed from the engine. Everyone in the pits held their breath as the dying 956 rolled over the finish line to win – some say the engine stopped right at this moment.

— White plumes of smoke trail the Porsche 956 and signal the death of the engine. But Hurley Haywood, Al Holbert and Vern Schuppan reach the line just ahead of their fast approaching teammates.

BP
BP PILOTE
Rothmans

# 20_ Le Mans 1988

*Well driven, lost by a whisker*

Porsche wanted to prove a point again at Le Mans in 1988. Since late 1986, Weissach had done barely any development on the once unbeatable sports prototype 962 C, as the difficult Indy project in the USA tied up all resources. Still, at Le Mans in 1987, the 962 C had defeated the all-conquering Jaguars that dominated the world championship. The 24 Heures were and remained the most important race of the year – for morale, for business, for everything.

In 1988, three 962 Cs went up against five Jaguars. The first skirmishes unfolded in qualifying, with Porsche eclipsing the competition: Hans-Joachim Stuck conquered pole position, six seconds faster than the best Jaguar. Works Porsches also occupied second and third place on the grid. However, as everyone knows, Le Mans is not decided during qualifying, or in the first few hours, during the night or in the final stages. Le Mans is won first and foremost in the preparation long before the start and then in every moment right up to the last seconds, as the number and range of possible mistakes and problems increase.

Two Jaguars put in a catapult start with two Porsches in hot pursuit. A fierce duel for the lead unfolded. In the third hour, Stuck's teammate Klaus Ludwig drove the tank empty. Using the starter motor, Ludwig coaxed the car back to the pits, losing seven minutes. At the halfway mark, Porsche seemed to be back in contention and was again running on the same lap as the leading Jaguar. Stuck turned the fastest lap of the race and retook the lead shortly after six o'clock in the morning. Then, a water pipe broke in the 962 C. After the repair, Stuck hurtled round the track in drizzle worlds faster than the rest of the field and was within 1:45 minutes of the Jaguar when his engine began to stutter. The Jaguar pulled away once more and increased the gap to six minutes. In the 22nd hour, Porsche undertook the risky task of changing the petrol filter. That did it! Now, the 962 C ran like a dream. Alas, it was too late. After their epic battle, Stuck, Derek Bell and Klaus Ludwig finished second, 2:36.9 minutes behind the victorious Jaguar.

___ The Porsche 962 C was the fastest car in the field in 1988, but an empty tank and a blocked fuel filter hampered the works car. After 24 hours, it fell short of victory by a mere 2:36.9 minutes.

DUNLOP
17
Shell
DUNLOP
DUNLOP
BOSCH

# 21 Le Mans 2017

*Going out with a bang*

In 1998, the works team had bid farewell to Le Mans after a dramatic double victory and then taken a break for 15 years. After a masterful comeback with wins in 2015 and 2016, it was time once again to say 'au revoir' in 2017. The factory outfit from Weissach did this in a most spectacular and entertaining way.

This time around, Toyota and Porsche were locked in the high-tech struggle twice around the clock. Three Toyotas versus two Porsches. The opening phase did not go well for the Germans, as the Japanese racing cars, which were actually built in Cologne, took the lead right from the start. After three and a half hours, the 919 Hybrid driven by Earl Bamber, Timo Bernhard and Brendon Hartley pitted to replace the front-axle drive. The Porsche remained stationary for 64 minutes and rejoined the race in 56th place, 13 laps behind the leader. When night fell, fortunes seemed to change: one Toyota dropped out with clutch problems, its sister car disappeared from the timing monitors after an accident. The third then retreated to the pits for hours. At 12:45am, Neel Jani, André Lotterer and Nick Tandy in the second Porsche took the lead and stayed there until, after more than 10 hours, engine trouble threw their 919 Hybrid out of the race.

Meanwhile, Bamber, Bernhard and Hartley had spent 15 crazy hours battling their way back up the order. All or nothing was the motto, and their car resolutely withstood the hellish tempo without any sign of problems. As Bernhard recalls: "When Brendon drove off after the repair, Earl and I started to calculate. We figured out that we could still make it to the podium. From that moment on, it was full throttle all the way.' With 66 minutes left, the Porsche overtook the leading Oreca prototype. And Porsche's farewell to Le Mans in 2017 turned into a triumph that had long seemed impossible. At present, it is uncertain if or when the record-winner Porsche will return to compete for outright victory at the world's most prestigious endurance race.

Joy after an unexpected win. The Kiwis Brendon Hartley (left) and Earl Bamber on the roof, Timo Bernhard with the black-and-red helmet sitting in the 919 Hybrid.

ROLEX
ROLEX
ROLEX
ROLEX
37
DMG MORI
DMG MORI
24h LE MANS
2
HY
P1
Mobil 1
MICHELIN
Mobil 1
MICHELIN
DMG MORI
CHOPARD
DMG MORI
CHOPARD

When a high top speed was called for, the long-tail racers took to the track. In this case, Richard Attwood and Vic Elford's 908 LH at Monza, 1969. Elford walks in front of the car.

# SUPER LIGHT & LONG-TAIL

6
S-M 2439
PORSCHE

# 22_Porsche 356 Super Light

*46 hp, seven men, and a class win*

It was early summer 1951: Porsche, with a workforce of 251 employees at the Stuttgart headquarters, was the first German car manufacturer to enter the 24 Hours of Le Mans after the Second World War. The expedition team that left Zuffenhausen for France was modest in size. Along with Paul von Guilleaume, the head of racing, there was Georg Heinemann as timekeeper, the mechanics Herr Briem and Herr Heiner, and Hans Klauser, head of customer service.

The 356 was the first German sports car to feature the SL designation for 'super light'. The coupés for Le Mans were part of the small production run from Gmünd in Austria, where Porsche had built its first sports cars between 1948 and 1950. At Stuttgart, 11 of these Gmünd coupés were converted into 356 SLs weighing 635 kilos. Producing 46 hp from a 1,086 cc engine with a double down-draught carburettor, reworked cylinder heads and a special camshaft, this 'aluminium can' could reach a speed of 160 kph. The 356 SL for Le Mans featured a more powerful alternator, a 68-litre tank, a longer axle ratio, lighter wheels, two throttle cables, double fuel pumps and petrol filters. The underfloor and the wheel casings had cladding, and a special racing seat provided 'firm support for the driver's hips', as recommended by an internal document. A windscreen washer system, wipers that could be worked by hand in an emergency and fog lamps were intended to provide good visibility in all weather conditions. Tricks such as the simultaneous operation of two 'fast-jacks' were to shorten the pit stops (in internal communications the pits were still called 'depots').

In practice, the racing driver Rudolph Sauerwein wrote off the 356 SL that he and Frenchman Robert Brunet were to drive, leaving him with a broken leg. In the second No. 46 'aluminium can', the French drivers Auguste Veuillet and Edmonde Mouche covered 2,840.65 kilometres in the race and won the 1.1-litre class.

June 23, 1951: the story of Porsche at Le Mans began with the 356 SL. Thanks to good aerodynamics, the 'aluminium can' reached 160 kph with just 46 hp – and finished as winner in its class.

# 23_Porsche 550 Prototype

*A message from reckless days*

Porsche aficionados are aware that Zuffenhausen entered a mid-engine car at Le Mans for the first time in 1953. It was the 550 prototype with a hardtop, significantly lighter than the 356 SL that competed in 1951 and 1952, more streamlined and a little faster than 200 kph with an 80 hp, 1.5-litre engine based on a Volkswagen motor. Young Hans Herrmann shared driving duties with the experienced Helmut "Helm" Glöckler in one of the 550s, while the second vehicle was driven by the Belgian journalist Paul Frère and Porsche's pressman-cum-factory driver Richard von Frankenberg. The petit Porsches scored a double victory in their class.

What some Porsche fans may not know is that Frankenberg wrote a humorous report for the customer magazine Christophorus. Today it reads like a message from reckless days. 1953 was long before the advent of safety cars, which now rein in the field after an accident or if the weather turns nasty. Although there were two serious crashes, the race continued at full speed. Through the infamous fog at Le Mans with zero viz, on the straights, drivers stuck to the lines in the middle of the track. But as for corners: '...Approaching the corner, we'd turn in at a grassy patch that we'd memorised... I think it's best I don't tell you how fast we drove.' Communication was mechanical rather than by radio. When the Porsche hurtled past the pits, a mechanic held up a 'P' sign. The driver then knew that there would be a message on a pit board on the following lap: 'refuel', 'drive faster' or 'slower'. Unbelievably, the Porsches covered 3,332 kilometres at an average speed of 138.8 kph on a single set of tyres. The drivers demonstrated true grit in what we'd now call 'simpler times'. While nutritionists and physiotherapists today look after the racing athletes, in the fifties the chauffeurs would just grab a hard-boiled egg or a chicken drumstick. And instead of a massage followed by a rest in an air-conditioned cabin, Frankenberg & Co. curled up in the seat of a Porsche in the car park. While sleep evaded them, at least they could enjoy the promenade of passing '... film stars, industrialists, and kings and queens of fashion...' as Frankenberg recalled.

The works 550 prototype driven by Helmut Glöckler and Hans Herrmann at Le Mans in 1953. The coupé was perfect. When it came to refreshments and sleep, each driver had to improvise.

44
44
PORSCHE

# 24_ Porsche 718 W-RS Spyder

*Forever young*

Porsche made about 80 units of the 718 between 1958 and 1962. Few cars created in Zuffenhausen were more versatile than this small space-frame racer with its light aluminium body. It raced as a Spyder or with an open glassed-in cockpit, as a coupé, as well as in Formula 1 and 2 versions. The first Porsche to clinch a top-three finish at Le Mans was a 718 RSK in 1958. The 718 won the Targa Florio more often than any other Porsche: in 1959, 1960 and 1963. The first overall victory at Sebring was scored in 1960 with a 718 RS 60. Between 1958 and 1964, Porsche drivers won the European Hillclimb championship every year but one – yes, you guessed it, in 718s. They were powered by Fuhrmann engines with a capacity of 1.5 to 2 litres and put out 150 to 185 hp. Two 718s even featured eight-cylinder, Type 771 engines.

One of these racing cars is a true celebrity, and no self-respecting book on Porsche would be complete without mentioning it: the 718 W-RS Spyder, produced in 1961 and, according to its chassis number, the last 718 made for the works racing team. An extended wheelbase provided space for an eight-cylinder engine, but in its first year, the W-RS Spyder was still powered by four cylinders. In 1961, it achieved second place in the Targa Florio and victory in its class at Le Mans, then still named 'RS 61'. In 1962, it tackled the World Endurance Trophy (that's the 'W' in its designation) with eight cylinders, a 2-litre engine and up to 240 hp, and was then entered for hill climbs in the USA. Two years is a long lifespan for a works racing car – but not for number 047, which the mechanics lovingly called 'grandmother'.

In 1963, 'grandmother' came to Le Mans as the first Porsche with fibreglass doors and bonnet. This time she was cantankerous, losing a back wheel. The driver, Edgar Barth, pushed her to the pits and took the chequered flag in eighth, absolutely exhausted. 'Grandma' rewarded Barth for his labour of love by winning the European Hillclimb Championship the very same year with him at the wheel. After repeating this success in 1964, 'grandmother' finally retired to the Porsche Museum.

A photo dating from 1962. The 718 W-RS Spyder with chassis number 047 had already been racing for two years – a ripe old age for a works car, but 'grandmother' continued for two more years.

F
111

# 25_ Porsche 906 Carrera 6

*Fast beauty*

Less weight, less air resistance, more power. This was the course that Porsche's visionary head of development, Ferdinand Piëch, set for the new 906 Carrera 6 in 1965. The weighing scales became a key instrument. The space frame made from 30 metres of steel tubing weighed just 53 kilos. Pedals, switches, covers and cladding were drilled, thinned down or discarded. A hole was even drilled in the ignition key. The works cars tipped the scales a little under 616 kilos, while those available to customers at a cost of 45,000 Deutschmarks were still below 700 kilos. A racing version of the still-young 2-litre 911 engine delivered power and a heavenly sound. Thanks to the use of materials like light alloy and titanium, the air-cooled flat-six weighed 130 kilos, 54 less than its series-production counterpart. With two triple carburettors, output reached 210 hp; with injection, 225. For truly serious cases, the 2.2-litre, eight-cylinder was available, generating 270 hp.

In view of such numbers, front-axle lift was unwelcome. The test department had a solution: rods projected out of the front wings from the upper wishbones through drilled holes. These rods were painted a different colour every two centimetres. If the front lifted during a test drive, the colours disappeared one by one. The driver reported what he saw, and the test team made spoilers to fit the situation. The 906 also spent a number of hours in the wind tunnel, leading to Porsche's first long-tail racing car for extremely fast tracks like Le Mans. It was more streamlined and faster than its short-tail cousin but would alarm the driver at 280 kph with the rear end becoming very, very light. Two spoilers helped keep the rear wheels from spinning in fourth gear.

The car's greatest success was an overall victory at the Targa Florio in 1966. At the end of the year, Zuffenhausen celebrated victory in the 2-litre class in the World Sportscar Championship. Customers campaigned the 906, of which 65 were produced, until the 1970s. To this day, fans admire the daring technology and the unique aesthetics of the 906.

__ A Porsche 906 long-tail at the Nürburgring in 1967. At the wheel, Swiss driver Rico Steinemann, who became the head of press relations and nominal head of racing at Porsche from 1969.

P
26

Gerhard Mitter won the 1966 GP of Hockenheim driving the factory's #1 906 long-tail. Günther Klass finished second in the work's #2 906 short-tail

CINZANO
CINZANO
CINZANO
CINZANO
2

# 26_ Porsche 907

*270 kph on the Salzburg Autobahn*

There's no way around the Porsche 907 in this book - for very good reasons. The legendary Jo Siffert drove his first race for the works team at Le Mans in 1967 in the brand-new long-tail 907. Siffert shared the cockpit with Hans Herrmann, and the pair won the 2-litre class for prototypes. With a drag coefficient of 0.27, the long-tail 907 was the most streamlined of all Porsches at that time and reached an amazing 302 kph down the long straight with a six-cylinder boxer producing 225 hp.

The teardrop-aerodynamics of the roof with its tinted see-through engine cover was retained for the 908 and up to the early 917s. In 1968, the 907 was the first Porsche endurance racing car with a space frame made of aluminium, which meant considerable savings in weight compared to steel. It was also the first in which the driver sat on the right – an improvement to weight distribution, as most racetracks are driven clockwise. Now powered with 270 hp from a 2.2-litre, eight-cylinder engine, it scored a sensational triple victory at the season-opening world championship event in Daytona, followed by a one-two at the 12-hour race at Sebring. Vic Elford and Umberto Maglioli won the Targa Florio in Sicily in a short-tail 907. In blistering form, Elford drove eight of the ten 72-kilometre laps, each with about 800 bends.

After a little more than a year, the story of the 907 as a works racing car concluded with a class win at Spa at the end of May 1968. So much for the history. To be honest, part of the reason we included the 907 in our little book was so we could show this wonderful photo. It was taken in 1967 on the Salzburg Autobahn, an Austrian federal highway between Anif and Salzburg. Peter Falk, head of pre-development and racing car development, took the wheel himself in order to determine the top speed of the long-tail 907 in the lead-up to the 24 Hours of Le Mans. Falk achieved a speed of more than 270 kilometres per hour. A golden age, a crazy age.

A test drive with the long-tail 907 on an Austrian Autobahn in 1967. According to reliable sources, the chief racing engineer Peter Falk reached 270 kilometres per hour.

S 993

# 27_ Porsche 908/02 Spyder

*The first world champion*

In the late 1960s, Porsche set a breathtaking pace in the development of racing cars. Zuffenhausen tackled the World Championship for Makes in 1969 with the 908, the 917 and the 908/02 Spyder. The 917 became a legend. Yet it was the 908/02 that won the manufacturer's title for Porsche – their first Spyder after the works squad had put its money on coupés for years with the 904, 906, 910, 907 and 908. It was also the first Porsche with a space frame that could be filled with pressurised air. Falling air pressure meant: We've got a crack somewhere.

Built to comply with the 1969 regulations for prototypes, the Spyder weighed 600 kilos, 70 kilos less than the long-tail 908. 73 centimetres high and 1.83 metres wide, the 908/02 looked spectacular. A healthy 360 hp from its eight-cylinder engine propelled the long-tail to 320 kph. The short-tail version for seriously twisty circuits recorded a top speed of 288 kph.

The Spyder premiered on March 22, 1969, with third place at Sebring and proceeded to collect laurels by the armful in the months to come: a triple victory at the Brands Hatch championship round, and the first four places at the Targa Florio. Moreover, a 908/02 with especially smooth bodywork secured a one-two result on the Nürburgring Nordschleife. It soon earned the nickname 'Flounder'. At Le Mans, the 'Flounder' set the third-fastest time in practice but retired with an overheating gearbox. On July 12, victory in the six-hour race at Watkins Glen was the last triumph for the works-run 908/02 Spyder. But customers continued to race the 908/02 into the mid-1970s. One of the most prominent was Steve McQueen, who scored second in the 12-hour race at Sebring in 1970 in a 'Flounder' with Peter Revson. McQueen also used this 908/02 as a camera car for his famous racing movie shot at Le Mans. The 'Flounder' still enjoys cult status among Porsche connoisseurs, and it lived on in the lines and proportions of open racing cars such as the 908/03 and 917 PA Spyder.

Brian Redman lets a 908/02 Spyder fly at the Nürburgring in 1969. He won the 1,000-kilometre race together with Jo Siffert. The 908/02 was Porsche's first Spyder after a long period of closed coupés.

OSTERREICH 2

A Porsche 908/02 Spyder in 1969. Weighing only 600 kilos with a 360 hp engine, this racing car won four events in the International Championship for Makes that year, securing the title for Porsche.

MARTINI
PORSCHE

# 28_ Porsche 935

*Read the rules, win the race*

In the 1976 World Championship for Makes, racing cars had to be based on production sports cars. This meant that the engineers had to read the rule books very, very closely: Where can I find a loophole that could save a few fractions of a second? Norbert Singer was in charge of conceiving the 935 at Porsche and found wriggle room in the rule that the wings could, within limits, be designed freely. The whole front of the 911, including the front wings, was a single component. So, the Singer crew smoothed out the torpedo tubes of the headlights, and the 'flat-nose' 911 with improved aerodynamics was born. In 1977, Singer turned his attention to the rear window. Its steep pitch caused the air stream to break away early, resulting in turbulence and increased air resistance. The regulations stated that the original rear window must be visible, but there was no mention of putting a flat window over it – which is exactly what Singer did.

The turbocharged 2.85-litre engine produced around 590 hp in 1976, and with two turbochargers in 1977, the figure increased to 680 horsepower. The 935 became much faster, and Porsche now also supplied the 970-kilogram car to customers, who raced it with great success. In 1977, the race department created the 935 2.0 'Baby', a super-light version mounted with a 1.4-litre turbo engine for the German Racing Car Championship. A year later, the extraordinary 935/78 took a whopping 800 hp to the starting line and reached just under 370 kph.

Customers and partners such as Andial, Brumos, Fabcar, Joest and Kremer Racing designed their own variations, collecting lots of laurels and trophies along the way. Hardcore 911 fans can recite the list of triumphs: four straight make's world championships from 1976 to 1979. The first win at Le Mans for a rear-engine racing car in 1979, while in the USA, the 935 won the IMSA GT Series from 1978 to 1982. Customer teams won the 24 Hours of Daytona with their 935s without interruption from 1978 to 1983, and at Sebring, the car scored six overall wins between 1978 and 1984. Accordingly, the 935 is still the most successful international racing version of the 911.

A Porsche 935 on the Nürburgring in 1976. Designed on the basis of the 911 after studying the rules closely, the 935 was one of the most successful racing Porsches in history.

MARTINI RACING
MARTINI PORSCHE
MARTINI PORSCHE.
1
MARTINI
Turbolader
BILSTEIN
BOSCH
Shell
DUNLOP

The works Porsche 935 arriving at the pits during the 1976 24 Hours of Le Mans. This extreme 911 with up to 850 hp scored several class wins and one overall victory at the endurance classic.

MARTINI PORSCHE
MARTINI
MARTINI RACI
40
Shell
MARTINI RACING

# 29_ Porsche 936 Spyder

*Bullseye at first shot*

In summer 1975, the racing department was redlining constantly to get their Porsche 935 ready for the 1976 World Championship for Makes. It was already August when Porsche boss Ernst Fuhrmann surprised his engineers with the idea of also entering a sports prototype in the World Sportscar Championship. A 935 and a prototype that doesn't even exist? Incredulity and amazement: that's impossible. 'No it's not', said the boss, and his men set to work. Suspension parts and wheels were still left over from the 917. The 2.1-litre engine with a turbocharger and 520 hp came from the 1974 911 Carrera RSR Turbo 2.1. The bodywork was first designed solely on the basis of sound judgement and experience. The front end was reminiscent of the 908/02, while the rear was more of a nod to the 917/30. The frame was new, and much to everybody's surprise, the hurriedly cobbled-together 765-kilo package worked beautifully: Porsche beat Renault at Le Mans in 1976, at the same time scoring the first win for a turbocharger and for a boxer engine at the famous endurance race. The 936 went on to win the World Sportscar Championship by a considerable margin.

In 1977, Porsche ran the 936 only at Le Mans – with new long-tail bodywork and two turbochargers on the six-cylinder engine, for which Porsche modestly admitted 540 horsepower. In the final minutes, victory over the mighty Renault fleet hung by a thread but was ultimately achieved. Water-cooled, four-valve heads and 580 hp were not enough to prevent a win by arch-rival Renault a year later, after the fifth gear failed in the two 936s. With no serious opposition in sight for the 936 in 1979, great optimism prevailed. However, the two cars entered did not make it to the finish at Le Mans – and ended up in the museum. Until, at the behest of the new Porsche boss Peter W. Schutz, they were wakened from their slumber and sent back to Le Mans in 1981. This time with more power than ever before. The six-cylinder, turbocharged motor, built for the single-seater Indy P6B, put out at least 630 hp from a 2.65-litre capacity. And from its fifth start at Le Mans, the 936 claimed its third victory. Not bad for a racing car that initially no one really wanted.

— The first weekend in April 1976: the 936 prototype, driven by Rolf Stommelen, makes its premiere at the Nürburgring. The racing department had improvised this prototype and it went on to win Le Mans three times.

MARTINI
BOSCH
Shell

# 30_ Porsche 961

*Treading a fine line*

René Metge and his co-driver Dominique Lemoyne won the world's toughest rally from Paris to Dakar in a Porsche 959 in January 1986. An unbelievable achievement, as this Porsche represented the technology of the future, with sequential turbocharging, variable four-wheel drive and chassis settings chosen by the driver.

The 959s had only just returned to Swabia from West Africa and the resilient racing department was still trying to catch up on sleep when the next adventure began: another version of the 959, with type number 961, was to be entered for Le Mans. From the Sahara to the Departément Sarthe – it was quite a stretch to cover all these bases. The 2.85-litre twin-turbo was souped up to 640 hp by raising the charging pressure. Aerodynamics was clearly an issue when tackling the six-kilometre straight and the super-fast Porsche Curve of the 'Circuit du Mans'. The racing department adopted a large rear wing and a massive front apron. The 961 eventually reached a top speed of 340 kph and cornered nicely. During early testing, the four-wheel-drive had pushed over the front axle, but the team around engineer Kussmaul got a grip on the nasty understeer by adjusting the suspension, the torque and weight distribution as well as the aero kit.

At Le Mans, René Metge took turns at the wheel of this one-of-a-kind vehicle with his French compatriot Claude Ballot-Léna, and once again Porsche made history at the 24-hour race: the 961 was the first four-wheel-drive to ever complete the marathon race. 321 laps and seventh place overall was significantly better than the racing department could have dreamed of from a production racer in a field of very special prototypes. A year later, the 961 started at Le Mans again with an improved chassis and a power boost to 680 hp. This time, however, fortunes did not favour the team from Weissach. The Porsche, driven by the naturalised Canadian Kees Nierop, spun into the barriers and burned out on lap 199.

Never before had a four-wheel-drive car completed the race at Le Mans. René Metge and Claude Ballot-Léna took seventh place in the 961 in 1986 – a brilliant result for a daring experiment.

C. BALLOT-LENA
speedline
180
Shell
BILSTEIN
BOSCH
SCHMITTHELM
Turbolader
KKK
PORSCHE
PORSCHE

The Porsche 961, a racing version of the Porsche 959 with 640 hp and a top speed of 340 kph, took seventh place in the 24 Hours of Le Mans in 1986.

PORSCHE
180
PORSCHE
Shell
PORSCHE
DUNLOP
DUNLOP

# 31_Porsche 962 IMSA

*Born for the USA*

The prototype 956 won every race in the World Endurance Championship for Makes in 1983. Now, the American IMSA GTP championship feared similar domination on home territory and bolted the gates by means of technical regulations. Porsche reacted by rebuilding the 956 for the American rule books: a wheelbase 12 centimetres longer, narrower tyres, a steel cage, a single turbocharger, and a larger tank. This was type number 962.

The new model made its debut in America in February 1984. It soon became clear that the huge downforce of the Porsche suited the twisty US tracks. But the air-cooled, 2.8-litre turbo engine lacked punch exiting the corners. The Porsche specialist Andial in California knew how to fix this problem with huge support from Porsche man Valentin Schäffer. At Andial, 1946-born Alwin Springer led the quest for horsepower at the time: 'The first thing we did was to enlarge the engines from 2.8 to 3.2 litres. But we wanted more than that. Although we had a great relationship with Weissach, they kept the lid tight on the key topic: Motronic. I looked for help in Silicon Valley, studied the electronics for six months and discovered how I could influence the boost, the ignition, the revs and the mix. That was a decisive step for achieving higher torque and performance. With Schrick and Mahle, we developed new shapes for pistons and combustion chambers after IMSA banned our double ignition. Garrett made compressor wheels for us. We reduced the distance for the inlet airflow between the charger, the intercooler and the engine. This improved the throttle response of the engine massively.'

Around 680 hp and 700 Newton-metres for an 850-kilo Porsche proved excellent ingredients for success: Porsche won the manufacturer's championship each year from 1985 to 1987. Al Holbert was crowned champion racing the 962 in 1985 and 1986, with Chip Robinson repeating this feat in 1987. From 1989, the 962 could be run with a double turbocharger, four-valve engine and water cooling. Nevertheless, the car's star was now on the wane, as new racing car concepts were coming to the fore.

___ The first 962 for the USA. Customers won the IMSA drivers' championship three times straight from 1985 to 1987, and Porsche was victorious in the manufacturer's championship from 1985 to 1988. 680 hp was clearly enough for 850 kilos.

PORSCHE
Shell
1
PORSCHE
Shell
PORSCHE
Shell
PORSCHE
BOSS
BOSCH
SCHMITHELM
BILSTEIN
speedline
TELETRON

# 32__Porsche 911 Turbo S Le Mans GT

*A new start with GT*

The World Sportscar Championship with 3.5-litre Formula 1 engines faded quietly away in 1992 due to lack of interest on the part of the manufacturers. So, 1993 brought the opportunity to chart new courses in endurance racing. The starter field for the 24 Hours of Le Mans gives colourful proof of the wide range of possibilities: Prototypes with 3.5-litre normally aspirated engines, old group C racing cars, new Le Mans prototypes and, for the first time since 1984, Gran Turismo racing cars rolled onto the grid.

Porsche set its sights on the GT class as the one with the best prospects for the future and decided to design a racing car based on the 911 Turbo S Lightweight. Out came the 911 Turbo S Le Mans GT, of which two were handbuilt. This über-911 was powered by a twin-turbo engine, reduced from 3.6 to 3.16 litres. With 35-millimetre restrictors, the flat-six put out 480 horsepower. Compared to its series-production counterpart, the racing car shed 390 kilograms thanks to the bonnet, front lid, doors, wings and aprons made of plastic. So, thanks to slimming down and clearing out – its weight was exactly one tonne. Air intakes behind the doors led to the brakes, and the air-air intercooler was fed fresh air through two openings in the very wide rear wing (getting the wing road-legal turned out to be a real feat). The rule book limited tyre width to 12 inches, requiring maximum sensitivity on the throttle pedal considering the turbopower on offer.

Hurley Haywood, Walter Röhrl and Hans-Joachim Stuck won their class at the first outing of the Turbo S LM GT at Sebring in 1993. At Le Mans, the trio set the benchmark for GTs until lap 79, when Röhrl retired after becoming entangled in an accident. The French Larbre Compétition squad acquired the car, finished second in the 24 Hours of Daytona in 1994, and won four more important GT races. A number of technical ideas that whizzed around racetracks in the Turbo S LM GT lived on successfully in the 911 GT2.

__ These guys go to the wall! Jean-Pierre Jarier, Jacques Laffite and Bob Wollek won the 1994 three-hour race at Zhuhai, China, in the 911 Turbo S Le Mans GT.

larbre compétition
86
GITANES
BLONDES
金美女
larbre compétition
SILEC
MICHELIN
elf
RAGUES

# 33_ Porsche 962 Dauer LM GT

*A slight problem with the '4'*

It was autumn 1993, and a lot of head-scratching was going on in the racing department. The issue was Le Mans, where prototypes with Formula 1 engines would probably be competing for overall victory. Porsche didn't have such an engine. In the class for 'large' Gran Turismo cars, Porsche's racing department expected McLaren to field a mid-engine racer. This meant that their own rear-engine 911 hardly stood a chance.

But the Porsche team spotted a glimmer of hope on the horizon: the former private team boss and racing driver Jochen Dauer had presented a sports car based on the successful Porsche 962 C prototype. Now the thought was: What if we get road traffic approval, as the regulations demand, develop the car further, and race it at Le Mans as a large GT? The management board gave the go-ahead, and on March 15, 1994, the 962 Dauer Le Mans GT received its road homologation. The last of many obstacles was the authorities' computer, which initially refused to allow the official top speed to begin with a four: 402 kph. Since autumn, the racing department had developed the competition version of the Porsche 962 Dauer. It was based on the 962 C and adapted to GT regulations with narrower tyres, an even underfloor between the axles and smaller diffusers, as well as a 120-litre tank and a weight of 1,000 kilos. The 3-litre, twin-turbo engine was adopted from the 962 C and generated 680 hp with restrictors.

In April, the organisers of the 24-hour race approved the car's entry, although with some reservations: this was a racing car turned into a road sports car, then converted into another racing car by the Porsche team – not something the French had envisaged. Porsche's two 962 GT were the big surprise of the race, rivalling a Toyota prototype for victory in a non-stop sprint. Tension skyrocketed in the pits from the fifth hour on, as the left-hand drive shafts of the 962 LM GT were overheating. But Porsche kept up the pressure on the Toyota and was ready to pounce when the leader ran into gearbox problems 90 minutes from the end. Finally, the Porsche 962 Dauer LM GT, driven by Mauro Baldi, Hurley Haywood and Yannick Dalmas, harvested the 13th overall victory at Le Mans for Porsche.

— The 1994 Le Mans winner during restoration at Porsche. The ex-prototype's race homologation as a 'Gran Turismo' was a techno-political masterstroke.

FATurbo-EXPRESS
F.A.T. INTERNATIONAL
Shell
36
FATurbo-
EXPRESS
PORSCHE
SACHS
GOODYEAR
DAUER
F.A.T. INTERNATIONAL
GROUPAGES EUROPÉENS
35
Shell
7
EINE KÖNIGIN UNTER DEN BIEREN
HAZET

# 34_ Porsche 919 Hybrid Evo

*Thunderous swansong*

Neel Jani, a Swiss with Indian roots, has been a professional racing driver for quite a while. He drove Champ Cars, was a Formula 1 test driver, and has won both the 24 Hours of Le Mans in a Porsche 919 Hybrid in 2016 and the World Endurance Championship WEC. If a professional like Neel feels awestruck, there has to be a special reason. Such a moment came when Jani tested the 919 Hybrid Evo. In a reverent tone, he told a British journalist: 'You – as the human – are at the limit. Not this car.'

Conceiving the 919 Hybrid Evo, Porsche's race engineers wrote a thunderous swansong for the 919 Hybrid, which had won Le Mans and every endurance world title in 2015, 2016 and 2017. For a farewell tour of legendary racetracks in early summer 2018, they abandoned all regulatory restrictions. The power of the 2-litre, four-cylinder turbo engine grew from 500 to 720 hp, while the e-motor on the front axle remained at 440 horsepower: 1,160 hp for a car weighing 849 kilos. This alone sounds fairly promising. A glance at the aerodynamics reveals a radical approach. The new front end, larger diffusers, the big wing extending far behind the rear and a great deal of detailed work added up to 50 per cent more downforce. Top speed was 369 kph. And then there were the electronics: the torque vectoring system with four wireless brakes prevented sliding and took the Evo through bends as if on rails.

On April 11, 2018, Jani steeled himself and tackled the high-speed circuit at Spa-Francorchamps in Belgium. The stopwatches recorded 1:41.77 minutes, eight-tenths of a second faster than the best Formula 1 lap at that time. Timo Bernhard added a fabulous time on the North Loop of the Nürburgring (our story 36). It was an emotional moment for the racing department when the 919 Hybrid fleet, led by Mark Webber in the 919 Hybrid Evo, drove along the country road from Weissach to the museum at Zuffenhausen on October 25, 2018, and Porsche concluded a dramatic chapter in racing history.

___ The works driver Neel Jani (with the pit board), the team and the 919 Hybrid Evo after his record lap at Spa in April 2018. Obviously, adrenaline makes you happy.

41
HÖRMANN
CHOPARD
SCHAEFFLER
PORSCHE
PORSCHE
919 tribute
919 hybrid
1
24h LE MANS
1
Esso
Mobil 1
SCHAEFFLER
CHOPARD

Drivers' rendezvous at Le Mans in 1988: (from left to right) Derek Bell, Klaus Ludwig, John Andretti, Michael Andretti, Hans-Joachim Stuck, Sarel van der Merwe, Bob Wollek and Mario Andretti.

# RACERS & GENTLEMEN

NISSAN
NISSAN
NISSAN
PORSCHE
Shell
Shell
DUNLOP

# 35 Stefan Bellof

*Speed and laughter*

A mop of blond hair, a winning smile, a mischievous spirit, and a fearless daredevil on the racetracks. Stefan Bellof's first race for Porsche was at Silverstone in 1983. The German out-qualified the rest by a full two seconds, leaving the world's best prototype racing drivers speechless.

There was only one thing that Stefan Bellof wanted: to leave everyone else in his dust. In the words of engineer Norbert Singer: 'Bellof drives everything like he's contesting Formula 1.' This was not exactly what you'd expect from an endurance driver, but his teammates accepted it. The older Derek Bell compensated for the young hotspur's fuel consumption with his gentler style in the cockpit of the 956. At the second round on the Nürburgring, Bellof tried Bell's patience severely. His practice lap of 6:11.13 – an average of over 200 kph on the Nordschleife – sent a shiver down the spine of everyone who had ever driven fast there. In the race, Bellof and Bell held a convincing lead until the young sprinter turned the 956 into a heap of wrecked metal and plastic. Bell was not amused.

Then came Le Mans: Jochen Mass and Bellof took turns at the wheel. Around midnight, the engine began to fade. Everyone was exhausted. And Bellof? Hans Eckert, a master mechanic in the racing department at the time, recalls: 'Stefan had fun in spite of all the problems. He repeatedly overtook two or three cars at the end of the straight, because he braked much later than they did. Then he came into the pits, laughing.' In 1984, Stefan Bellof divided his time between the Tyrrell Formula 1 team and Porsche – at the end of the year he was crowned the first German Endurance World Champion. 1985 was devoted to Formula 1, but on the Grand Prix-free weekends, he drove a 956 B belonging to his friend Walter Brun.

Bellof was 27 years old when he had a fatal accident during the 1,000-kilometre race in Spa-Francorchamps in 1985. His record for the Nordschleife was only broken in 2018 – by the World Endurance Champion and Le Mans winner Timo Bernhard in a Porsche 919 Hybrid Evo. One of Bernhard's great idols: Stefan Bellof.

Stefan Bellof: his record time for the Nordschleife, set in 1983, remained intact until 2018. In 1984, he became the first German Endurance World Champion. Everyone remembers his daredevil style and his contagious laugh.

# 36_ Timo Bernhard

*"Pretty fast"*

Born in 1981, 130 kilometres south-west of the Nürburgring as the crow flies, Timo Bernhard signed a contract as a Porsche junior racing driver in 1999. Young Bernhard was fast and blessed with an enormous feeling for his cars. And he was very determined. In hindsight he says: 'My fitness regime and my iron will to succeed were a bit too much of a good thing.' The first wins eased the pressure and Timo went on to win every championship he competed in, at first in Gran Turismo 911s, not to forget this five victories at the Nürburgring 24 Hours, as well as Daytona and Sebring.

But Timo found his true vocation in developing the RS Spyder prototype: 'I was involved with the development of the car. When I drove it for the first time in August 2005, I immediately saw that this high downforce prototype suited me best.' Downforce and power in abundance, that was the thing! Bernhard became champion in the USA with the RS Spyder in 2007 and 2008 and won Le Mans in 2010 in an Audi prototype. Then, in spring 2012, this happened: while testing at Sebring, Bernhard flew off the track at 300 kph with the Audi after suspension damage. A fractured cervical vertebra was one of many injuries. In retrospect, he reflects: 'My greatest achievement in motor racing might be that I fought my way back to top level.'

The development of the Porsche 919 Hybrid was another exceptional story. He drove the roll-out on June 12, 2013, became Endurance World Champion in 2015 and 2017 and won Le Mans in 2017. Coming from 56th position following a repair! The spectacular conclusion to his mission with the 919 came on June 29, 2018. Bernhard put in a devastating lap around the Nürburgring Nordschleife with the 1,100+hp, 849 kg 919 Hybrid Evo. The stopwatch recorded a time of 5:19.55 minutes; 51.6 seconds faster than the previous record. 'Pretty fast,' says Timo with a chuckle. In late 2019, Bernhard retired as a works driver. His two decades in the sport are still fresh in our memories and already provide the stuff of legends – about one of the friendliest people on this planet, who drove like the devil.

__ Timo Bernhard: one of the friendliest people in the world – and one of the fastest: Le Mans winner, World Endurance Champion, and holder of an unworldly record at the Nürburgring.

LKM
DMG MORI
CHOPARD
Porsche LMP Team
CHOPARD
DMG MORI
DMG MO
Mobil

# 37_Mark Donohue

*'Captain Nice' and the turbo revolution*

Mark Donohue drove a Porsche 917/10 Spyder with a 4.9-litre, twelve-cylinder turbocharged engine and about 850 hp for the first time on the Weissach test track on October 27, 1971. At the age of 34, 'Captain Nice' was a star in the USA, having won four national championships with Penske Racing. Penske and Porsche planned to compete in the American-Canadian Can-Am Series with the Spyder in 1972, and to run Porsche's turbo engine on the twisty US and Canadian circuits - a daring feat in the turbo stone age. Donohue threw himself into the development as a test driver and engineer, commuting ceaselessly between the USA and Weissach.

While developing with Porsche, he won the Indy 500 for Penske in a McLaren on May 27, 1972. While test-driving the 917/10 at Mosport shortly afterwards, Donohue pulverised the Formula 1 lap record. During testing at Road Atlanta on July 3, the incorrectly fitted rear bodywork flew off the 917/10 at 240 kph. Donohue survived the massive shunt with an injured knee but had to miss five races. George Follmer became champion in the 917/10, and Donohue noted that: 'What bothered me even more was seeing George drive this beautiful car, which I had developed just as I wanted it over many months. That's what it must be like to find another man in bed with your wife.' Donohue's comeback was difficult, and later he fondly reminisced about the whiskeys that he and Porsche boss Ernst Fuhrmann drank together in a motorhome at the circuit after defeat in a race.

Mark first tested the 917/30 for the 1973 season on December 15. It featured improved aerodynamics, a longer wheelbase and a 5.4-litre, twin-turbo engine producing 1,100 hp. The 917/30 was ready in time for the third race of the season. Donohue won every race (setting the fastest lap) from pole position and took the title. Can-Am subsequently banned Porsche by changing the rules. Donohue switched to Formula 1, but set a world record in a 917/30 (our story 97). On August 17, 1975, Donohue crashed during the warm-up for the Austrian F1 Grand Prix and died of brain injuries two days later.

Mark Donohue: the name of this racing driver and engineer will always be associated with the development and triumphs of the Porsche 917/30. This photo was taken at Riverside, USA, in 1973.

SUNOCO
PORSCHE
SUNOCO
Mark Donohue
TECH

# 38_ Paul Frère

*A speedy scribe*

Paul Frère was a top motoring writer and a very gifted racer whose skill behind the wheel impressed Porsche's Huschke von Hanstein so much, that the Count entrusted the writer-racer with one of the works 550 prototypes for Le Mans 1953. Frère drove the car to class victory with Richard von Frankenberg. This was the start of a relationship that Frère described in his autobiography, My Life Full of Cars, as a 'long, happy connection with Porsche.'

In 1958, in his second Le Mans for Zuffenhausen, Frère won the 1.5-litre class in a 718 RSK with Edgar Barth and finished fourth overall. He was not happy with this result. In his opinion, more would have been possible, but team orders had held him back, finishing one lap behind his teammates Jean Behra and Hans Herrmann in a 2-litre RSK. Behra and Herrmann finished third in the overall rankings and climbed the winners' podium.

Born to Belgian parents in 1917, Frère discovered his talent for driving late by today's standards and contested his first race at the Spa-Francorchamps circuit in 1948. For all his success, he regarded himself as a journalist who raced, not the other way round. Frère competed in 11 Grands Prix and won Le Mans in 1960 with Ferrari. After this triumph, he decided to dedicate all of his time to his typewriter. With a brilliant knowledge of his subject, Frère wrote many motoring books, including Porsche Racing Cars of the 70s, in which, to the surprise of the legendary team boss John Wyer, Frère revealed a number of details of the JWAE-run Porsches. His definitive work, however, is The Porsche 911 Story. It was in print continuously from 1976 until Frère's death in 2008 and was reprinted in 2013.

Many bends on the racing circuits of this world are named after famous drivers. But only one commemorates a motorsport journalist. A fast right-hander of the Circuit de Spa-Francorchamps in Belgium's Ardennes honours the memory of one of the greats of motorsport journalism as the 'Courbe Paul Frère'.

___ Paul Frère in the cockpit of a racing car in the late 1950s. His first race for Porsche at Le Mans in 1953 was the start of a 'long, happy connection'.

# 39_ Dan Gurney

*Racing history with a difference*

America's Dan Gurney joined Porsche Rennsport in 1961, and on July 8, 1962, he scored his – and Porsche's - first Formula 1 victory on the fast road circuit of Rouen-Les-Essarts in Haute Normandie at the French Grand Prix driving a Porsche Type 804. The only Formula 1 single-seater that Porsche ever made weighed 452 kilos with its steel space frame and aluminium bodywork. Its air-cooled, 1.5-litre, eight-cylinder flat engine made from light alloy metal put out 180 hp. Drivability was not particularly overwhelming with decent power between just 6,000 and 9,200 revs. The 804 was the first Porsche to feature disc brakes all round. All in all, a package with potential, but not one favoured by Ferry Porsche. After seven Grands Prix in 1962, the company moved on from Formula 1 racing.

Gurney re-oriented himself and continued to make history. He was the first driver to score wins in Formula 1, in sports car racing, in the American NASCAR and in IndyCars. In 1967, he triumphed at Le Mans at the wheel of a Ford GT40 MkIV. The team fashioned the now-famous 'Gurney bubble' on the roof of the GT40 for the 1.93-metre tall giant. From the podium, he showered Henry Ford with champagne – and the champagne shower tradition was born. From the next year on, Gurney put his mark on the Indy 500, finishing second twice and third once in 1968 to 1970. As team boss and designer of All American Racers, which he founded in 1966, he won the 1967 Belgian Grand Prix driving his own Eagle Weslake Formula 1. Gurney was the first driver to compete wearing a full-visor helmet in 1968. He won the Indianapolis 500 in 1973 while continuing to design and invent, among other things, the Gurney flap spoiler. His All American Racers has evolved into a high-tech company, which recently developed and manufactured parts for SpaceX rockets.

Through all the years and activities, Porsche stayed very close to Dan Gurney's heart: In 1969, he married the journalist and Porsche employee Evi Butz, and they stayed together until Dan Gurney died at the age of 86 in 2018.

Dan Gurney: a great racing driver, team owner and designer. In 1962, he won the French Grand Prix in a Porsche, and in 1969 married Evi Butz, a journalist and Porsche employee.

OPTICAL COMPANY

# 40_ Leo Kinnunen

*Words are silver, action is gold*

Leo Kinnunen rarely spoke about his legendary lap at the Targa Florio in 1970. Perhaps he shared his thoughts with his Finnish compatriots, perhaps with his sponsor and confidant Antti Aarnio-Wihuri (AAW). This is the way with many Nordic maestros of the steering wheel: as silent and hard as the granite of their homeland. It is said that they answer questions with the throttle pedal. They might even give statements with the right foot, for example: "I'm as fast as the team's number one... if you let me."

At the 1970 Targa, Leo drove a 908/03 – a slender 550 kilos with a 350 hp engine, an agile and fragile Porsche Spyder, which the world-class British team JWAE fielded for Porsche. As always, he shared the cockpit with superstar Pedro Rodríguez. This duo had already won three world championship events, but this time victory proved elusive. After Kinnunen had taken the lead from the start, Rodríguez, running a fever, took the wheel, but only managed a few laps and lost a lot of time. Leo took over and ploughed his way up the order. Then came the final 72-kilometre lap. Another 800 bends without a safety net, and the six-kilometre straight line along the ocean at full throttle. When this lap was over, Kinnunen had shoved Vaccarella/Giunti in their Ferrari from second place and set a record for eternity: 33 minutes and 36 seconds. Leo was faster than 'number one' Rodríguez, and faster than the rest of the world. 'Take note,' he would have thought (in Finnish, of course, as he preferred to express himself in his mother tongue).

Kinnunen went on to win the European Interserie with the AAW team's Porsche 917 and 900 hp 917/10 from 1971 to 1973 and also underlined his driving genius with third place at the Thousand Lakes Rally in a 911 Carrera RS in 1973. Never before and never since has a Porsche finished so high up the rankings at 'the Finnish Grand Prix'. In 1969, the Finn had caught the attention of the Porsche engineer Helmut Flegl during testing the 917. Flegl reported that: 'Kinnunen was the most dramatic drivers of all. He threw the car into the bends like the devil...' Drama, but in typical Finnish manner, in keeping with the motto: 'Words are silver, action is gold.'

___ Leo Kinnunen in 1972. The Finn underlined his skill in the 917/10 Spyder and in rally cars and put his name in the history books with a record lap at the 1970 Targa Florio in a 908/03.

40

The 1970 Targa Florio road race. Leo Kinnunen's lap record with the spectacular 908/03 still stands today.

# 41_ Gijs van Lennep

*Turning passion into history*

Gijsbert van Lennep followed his passion and went motor racing. Fortunately, his passion was combined with exceptional talent and a fair portion of courage. Born in 1942 into an aristocratic Dutch family, he climbed the ranks to race in Formula 1 and at the wheel of several of Porsche's finest racing cars.

Gijs, as he is known in the racing world, started his career in the 1960s driving Formula V and Formula 3. In 1966, the 'Racing for Holland' squad entrusted one of their Porsche 906 to the swift young man. By 1967, he was sitting in a works 911, and in 1970 won the very first Porsche Cup as the world's best private driver. In that same year, van Lennep took on Le Mans in a 917. He recalls the formidable 600-hp Porsche as a 'fantastic racing car... you could throw it around like a big go-kart,' and '... apart from that, as a young man, you are afraid of nothing.' His first outing in a 917 ended with a tyre bursting at 320 kph. Fortunately, the brave Dutchman emerged without a scratch. Twenty-five more starts with a 917 followed, a record that Gijs holds to this day.

In 1971, van Lennep won at Le Mans with Helmut Marko in the famous works-run short-tail 917 with a magnesium frame. Hampered by ailing brakes during the last three hours, the Dutchman and the Austrian pushed on, as repairs would have cost them victory. The distance record they set stood for decades. Emphasising his all-rounder qualities, van Lennep was also victorious at the 1973 Targa Florio with Herbert Müller in a 911 Carrera RSR. This win was special, too, as the Sicilian road race was run as a world championship event for the last time. A year later, van Lennep drove the first turbocharged Porsche at Le Mans, finishing second with Herbert Müller in a 911 Carrera RSR Turbo 2.1. Two years later, this time with Jacky Ickx, he chalked up the first win for a turbo racing car at Le Mans in a Porsche 936. Once again, the gentleman with his ever-friendly and relaxed manner had made history. At this point, Gijs decided to call it a day and hung up his racing helmet.

__ Gijs van Lennep (left) was one of the fastest Porsche racing drivers – here at an award ceremony in 1974 with (from left to right) Herbert Müller, Ferry Porsche and Manfred Schurti.

DAUERTEST MIT AUSZEICHNUNG BESTANDEN
PORSCHE
CARRERA TURBO
24 STUNDEN LE MANS 1974
CUP, 74
GELO
SUPER SPORTS CAR RACING 74
Final Results
MARTINI RACING
Shell

# 42_Jochen Mass

*Steely determination*

Blessed with a huge driving talent, an athletic physique to boot and, as a British motoring magazine put it, a steely determination. A self-assured cosmopolitan, a connoisseur of the good life. Jochen Mass, an ex-sailor from Bavaria, turned up in top-level motor racing in 1971 at the age of 25. By 1973, he had advanced to Formula 1, and in 1976, he joined Porsche where he spent almost a decade notching up victories and world championship titles – most of them with Jacky Ickx. On March 21, 1976, in Mugello, this duo – dubbed 'MIX' on the pit board – won Mass's very first race for Porsche at their first start.

That year, he switched effortlessly between the 935, the sports prototype 936 (five races, five wins) and Formula 1. Again and again, his steely determination shone through. Ickx burned the clutch of the 935 taking off from the grid at Silverstone. It took the Belgian and Mass 40 minutes to push the car back to the pits. After 55 minutes of repair work, Mass launched his charge through the field, promptly setting a lap record. The MIX duo was now the fastest in the field, racing to tenth place, as well as a place in the fans' hearts. 1977 began with a spirited drive at Daytona, slicing through the field from 42nd to second position, before retiring with tyre damage. The 935/78 appeared in 1978 – its handling not quite up to its 800 hp, according to Mass. But MIX won at Silverstone wrestling this monster. Over one single lap, Mass eked out a four-second advantage from the rest of the field. In spring 1982, Mass and Ickx conducted the first high-speed tests with the 956 at Le Castellet. Mass described this ground-effect Porsche as 'absolute magic'.

MIX contributed decisively to Porsche's World Endurance Championship titles from 1982 to 1985, and at times Mass's determination could only be tamed by means of extremely clear and direct communications. With fuel running low at the race at Monza in 1983, the team held up pit signs with the order to 'slow'. Mass, unimpressed, kept the throttle pedal down until the head of racing Peter Falk swung a hammer next to the sign. Jochen finally eased up, and MIX finished a close second.

— Jochen Mass's portrait on an autograph card. Mass was always friendly, fast, showed 'steely determination' and was blessed with the constitution of an ox.

# 43_Jackie Oliver

*'Close your eyes and hope for the best!'*

It was a duel that Porsche fans still talk about to this day: the 1,000 kilometres at Spa-Francorchamps in 1971. Two Porsche 917s campaigned for Zuffenhausen by the British JWAE team under John Wyer, fought valiantly wheel-to-wheel to the last minute. In the end, Jackie Oliver and Pedro Rodríguez won with an average speed of 249 kph, four-tenths of a second ahead of their teammates Derek Bell and Jo Siffert. When Jackie Oliver was asked at the Porsche Rennsport Reunion in 2015 how it was to take Eau Rouge at full throttle in a 917, he answered merrily: 'I haven't a clue. I just told myself: close your eyes and hope for the best!'

John Wyer knew the 29-year-old British driver well, as Jackie Oliver and Jacky Ickx had beaten the Porsche team in Wyer's Ford GT40 after an epic struggle at Le Mans in 1969 to win the marathon race. Porsche then contracted Wyer, and he brought Oliver along with him for 1971. The British driver and Rodríguez climbed to the top of the podium for the third time at Spa, having already won at Daytona and Monza sharing the 917. The pair was heading for victory again at Le Mans in a 600 hp 917 when a severed oil pipe ended their race at two o'clock in the morning. But Oliver had already put his name in the annals of this famous endurance race by turning a record-breaking lap in practice, with an average speed of 250.475 kilometres an hour.

After a successful 1971 campaign, Porsche, Wyer and Oliver parted company. Oliver turned his attention to the Can-Am Series, winning it in 1974 in a Shadow prototype. But Formula 1, where he had been involved on and off since 1968, was his true love. After his final race in a Shadow F1 in 1977, Oliver was one of a group of four Britons to leave the team and found their own squad under rather stormy conditions: the Arrows F1 team. But that is another story.

___ A proud moment: Jackie Oliver (right) and Pedro Rodríguez after winning at Monza driving a short-tail 917 in 1971.

Gulf

# 44_Brian Redman

*Triumph and near-tragedy*

His family produced mops, and the young Brian Redman, born in 1937 in the north-west of England, was proud of providing the fastest delivery service in the county. He also showed a talent for racing without mops and discovered his true vocation in 1966: endurance events.

Redman took the wheel of a works Porsche for the first time in 1969, forming a dream combination with Jo Siffert. Siffert was the full-throttle beast, Redman the lightning-fast finisher. The duo won five of ten world championship races, thus securing Porsche's first International Championship for Makes practically on their own. In the same year, Redman sampled the 917 for the first time, describing its early versions as rather uncontrollable and fragile. All the same, he and Richard Attwood braved the 12-cylinder beast to claim third place at Zeltweg. Asked for his highlight of 1970, Redwood left no room for doubt: victory with Jo Siffert in the Targa Florio driving the 908/03 following a hard-fought battle against Ferrari's Nino Vaccarella and Ignazio Giunti. Redman still raves about the 908/03: 'A wonderful car to drive. The Spyder was incredibly agile, had power and no ground effect. So you could throw the car into corners superbly.'

After these successes, Redman said goodbye to racing and became a Volkswagen dealer in South Africa. He stuck it out for four months, returned to England and answered John Wyer's call to drive a 908/03 in the Targa Florio in 1971. Triumph was then followed by near-tragedy. Redman drove the start and, possibly as a result of a defect, crashed into a concrete wall after half a lap. The car caught fire. Redman managed to escape, but was badly burnt and almost fell victim to the rudimentary medical care that was available at the track. That did not stop the likeable Briton from continuing racing and notching up more successes, including three F5000 titles between 1974 and 1976. He also collected accolades for Porsche, most notably winning Sebring driving a 935 in 1978, and the 24 Hours of Daytona in 1981. Brian then called it quits for good and moved to sunny Florida.

Brian Redman (right) with Jo Siffert after winning the 1970 Targa Florio. The Briton and the Swiss had secured the first International Championship for Makes for Porsche in 1969.

CHRONOMATIC
HEUER
Gulf
Gulf

# 45_Pedro Rodríguez

*Mexican revelation*

As long as he was not at the wheel of a racing car, Pedro Rodríguez acted: 'well-brought-up, quiet, usually friendly, but reserved to the point of secretiveness', as his driver colleagues described him. His team boss, John Wyer, found the Mexican very laid-back: 'If he can sit, he doesn't stand, and if he can lie down, he doesn't sit.' Rodríguez in the cockpit was a completely different story: fatalistic, fearless, resolute to the point of ruthlessness and sensationally talented.

In 1968, he won Le Mans with Lucien Bianchi in a Ford GT40 entered by John Wyer. Wyer brought him back into his JWAE team in 1970, where Rodríguez drove a Porsche 917 and a 908/03. The Swiss driver Jo Siffert was his toughest teammate. Until Rodríguez arrived, Siffert was considered number one and the fastest man in a racing Porsche. He then won four races in the World Sportscar Championship in 1970 and 1971, with Rodríguez victorious in eight. The Mexican-Swiss duel was one of the most intensely fought in racing history and there were times when John Wyer paired the two up in one of his cars just to make sure that a JWAE car would make it to the finish.

Rodríguez was a revelation in the rain. A stop-and-go penalty at Brands Hatch had set him back to 12th place. He then hustled the Porsche through the rain and fog, to win five laps ahead of the rest. In this race, his teammate Leo Kinnunen hardly got a stint at the wheel. The same thing happened to Richard Attwood in 1971 in the 1,000-kilometre race at Zeltweg in Austria, where Rodríguez drove 157 out of 170 laps – with his foot to the floor after a change of battery had cost the 917 three laps. The Mexican gained two laps on the leading Ferrari, and then the Italian car hit the barrier. Rodríguez won but was disappointed that he had not been able to beat the Ferrari fair and square. Two weeks later, Pedro Rodríguez suffered a fatal crash in a private Ferrari during the 200-mile race in Nuremberg. He was 31 years old.

___ Pedro Rodríguez in a Porsche 908/03 at the Nürburgring in 1970. The Mexican was regarded as a merciless opponent and was a revelation in the rain. His duels with Jo Siffert are legendary.

# 46_ Björn Waldegård

*Sensitive antennae*

Björn Waldegård from Sweden, born in 1943, a bear of a man, quiet and friendly in his reserved Scandinavian way. In 1967 and 1968, 'Walle' won the Swedish Rally Championship throwing underpowered VWs around the icy forest roads of his homeland. In the 1960s and 1970s, rally drivers from Scandinavia had a reputation for being fast on ice, snow and gravel. But on asphalt? Not really.

Then Waldegård joined the Porsche works team, starting out in 1969 at the Monte Carlo Rally in a Porsche 911 S, where he beat his teammate and the previous year's winner, Vic Elford. He was faster than the British driver on dry asphalt, on snow and on ice. The young Swede's drive caused a sensation. Waldegård won the 'Monte' again in 1970, as well as the Swedish and the Austrian Alpine rally. In the Targa Florio, he and Richard Attwood drove a 908/03 and finished fourth, took the flag in second place at the 86-hour Marathon de la Route on the Nordschleife of the Nürburgring with two colleagues in a 914/6, and then saved Porsche's honour by scoring third at the 'Monte' in 1971. Waldegård drove for Porsche until the works team withdrew from rallying in 1972. However, even after this official farewell, Zuffenhausen still pursued one aim: to win the prestigious Safari Rally through East Africa. Waldegård was famous for his sensitive antennae. He sensed what a car could take, and found his way through terrain that appeared impassable at first sight. But the rally gods weren't on his side, and despite four attempts, he failed to win the Safari Rally with a 911. Second place in 1972 was his best result.

Porsche was already concentrating on racing when Waldegård won the first-ever driver's world rally championship in 1979 with Ford and Mercedes. From 1977 to 1990, he won the Safari Rally four times with Ford and Toyota. After 20 victories at the highest international level, Waldegård retired from professional motorsport in 1992 – though not completely. He continued to contest historic events and soon gained a reputation as one of the fastest men around on vintage Porsches. In 2011, with his son Mathias in the co-driver's seat, he won the East African Safari Classic for historic rally cars. His vehicle: a 911. Björn Waldegård died in 2014.

__ Björn Waldegård at the Sweden Rally in 1969. Just prior to this, he had won the Monte Carlo Rally with his co-driver Lars Hjelmer and was obviously still in high form: he went on to win in his home country, too.

Gulf
3
BB 3020

July 1979: a model of the Porsche 935/80 'Moby Dick 2' in the wind tunnel. The aerodynamics was revolutionary, but the car was never built.

# VISIONS & WIND TUNNELS

# 47_ 914/6 Count von Görtz

*Exceptional aristocrat*

In the late 1960s, Ferry Porsche asked Count Albrecht von Görtz (1914–2006) to present his interpretation of the newly launched Porsche 914 mid-engine sports car.

Von Görtz had achieved well-earned fame as an automotive designer by creating the BMW 507 and had been invited by Porsche to present his idea for a successor to the 356, the Type 695, in the early 1960s. However, his proposal, with double headlights and other unorthodox elements, seemed all-too American for Porsche. No wonder: Count von Görtz had emigrated to the USA in 1935. He first made a living doing casual jobs, before attracting attention with his hot-rod car bodies. Two years as a designer at Studebaker followed before von Görtz opened his own studio. Here, he worked on the BMW 507, at the suggestion of the extremely active and influential automobile importer and visionary Max Hoffman, completing the styling in 1955.

Now it was time for an alternative 914. Von Görtz was given a 914/6 R – a racing version that is – as the starting point and basis for his work. According to legend, the Carozzeria Eurostyle in Turin morphed the racing car into a one-off prototype using sketches and a 1:5 model that the nobleman had created. The good count presented his version of the 914 in Zuffenhausen in 1970. His idea broke with many of the stylistic elements that were common at Porsche. The lines and the proportions seemed to go more in the direction of Lotus, Jensen and Ferrari. The front wings may be regarded as quoting the 911, but their wedge-like, edgy finish seemed more reminiscent of the then-popular Opel GT. It would appear that this design found initial favour in the eyes of Porsche, and it is claimed that brochures had already been printed when the decision was finally made to abandon the production of this 914 after all. But Count von Görtz obviously liked it – he went on to drive this unique prototype as his private car for several years.

__ The 914/6 as Count von Görtz presented it to Porsche. This bold proposal by the star designer caused a stir at the motor show in Turin in 1970, but only the single prototype was produced.

# 48_Porsche 916 Brutus

*Hefty power, hefty price*

You'll surely know the 1969 Porsche 914: pontoon styling, pop-up headlights, a three-seater with a removable plastic roof and a mid-engine producing 80 or 110 hp (as a 914/6). You might also know the 914/8, of which Porsche made two in 1969 for Ferry Porsche and Ferdinand Piëch. What followed marked the pinnacle of the 914 evolution: the 916. In 1971, 11 prototypes of this 914 on steroids were made, to put a shine on the image of the 'Volkswagen Porsche' – mainly on the racetracks. Three 916s were mounted with the 190 hp, 2.4-litre engine from the 911 S, and seven were powered by the 2.7-litre flat-six of the forthcoming Carrera RS producing 210 hp. But only one of them – the first – ended up with the 300 horsepower racing engine of the 911 Carrera RSR installed in front of the rear axle. The welded-in steel roof and a reinforced floor increased the rigidity of this unique prototype. The sports suspension with stiffer springs, special shock absorbers, inner-vented disc brakes and 180/17 VR 15 tyres matched the engine performance and provided very sporty handling.

These impressive specs are less surprising if one considers for whom the first 916 was conceived. It was the technical managing director and top motor racing manager of Porsche KG, Ferdinand Piëch. Piëch handed the mid-engine car on to his first wife Corina, whose name adorns the glove compartment (it wasn't their daughter Corina, born in 1960). Piëch's wife came up with a suitable name for the powerpack: Brutus. This lettering can be seen on the left-hand-side of the rear lid. On the right, the number '2.9' indicates the capacity of the six-cylinder engine.

An American soldier acquired Brutus in 1974 and took the Porsche back to the United States, where it was rediscovered decades later. After meticulous restoration work, Brutus turned heads as one of the more exotic items at an auction in Paris in February 2019. The gavel came down at the remarkable price of 906,000 USD, presumably making Brutus not only the most powerful but also the most expensive 914 ever made.

___ Brutus at the Werk 2, Stuttgart-Zuffenhausen, in 1973. The large front spoiler is by Style Porsche Design. The tyres in 180/17 VR 15 dimension was considered very wide at the time.

# 49__World-record Porsche 924

*Good for 280 kph – and never run*

The Porsche 924 arrived in showrooms in January 1976 and gave dyed-in-the-wool fans of the Stuttgart sports car manufacturer plenty to chew on: the water-cooled, four-cylinder, inline engine lived beneath the front bonnet. Four breaches of taboo under one lid! Moreover, the block of the 125 hp motor came from Volkswagen and the technology from Audi, where the 924 was manufactured. The media and fans wondered if this car really had what it took to fly the Porsche badge.

Porsche decided to dispel all doubts and ambiguities by means of a top sporting performance: the 924 was to run 10,000 miles at an average speed of 250 kph, which would have been a world record. So the racing department went to work. They doubled the output of the 2-litre engine to 250 horsepower with the help of a turbocharger. The very light bodywork was made from plastic, with only the essential air inlets, and a huge front spoiler. The car had neither wing mirrors nor solid door handles, and the wheels were partially covered. Air deflectors at the rear reduced turbulence and thus air resistance. The drag coefficient fell from 0.36 to 0.268 – a masterful achievement. The world-record hopeful weighed a mere 980 kilos and was capable of a top speed of 280 kilometres per hour.

The world record attempt was to be made on the Italian Nardò Ring high-speed test track in July 1977. Jacky Ickx, Jürgen Barth, Günter Steckkönig and Eberhard Braun were on the list of drivers, to be joined by the Americans Al Holbert and Peter Gregg. With the world-record 924 ready to go and the drivers on standby, the board of management decided against the attempt. And what could have been the fastest-ever 924 went from Weissach straight to the Porsche Museum.

In spite of all the initial pessimism, the 924 proved a reasonable success. Whether it was a genuine Porsche or not, a starting price just below 25,000 Deutschmarks, modest fuel consumption and a sporty performance convinced 150,684 purchasers to opt for the transaxle sports car by the time production ceased in 1988.

__ This 924 was tailor-made for a world-record attempt in 1977. Check out the very short side pipe at the front, the lack of wing mirrors, the partly covered wheels and the air deflector at the rear.

NOTAUSGANG

# 50_Porsche 924 Targa Concepts

*Open-air varieties*

The Targa – fans of the 911 have loved this concept right from day one. The idea of a removable plastic roof between the windshield and the massive roll bar had also contributed significantly to the 914's unique character. Hence, it seemed a good idea to also offer the Porsche 924 transaxle sports car featuring the fresh-air solution with the Mediterranean-sounding name.

In early summer 1977, Porsche engineers and stylists were busy weighing up their options: how do we realise a 924 Targa? All the head-scratching came to a promising end with a handful of highly attractive Type 941/942 concept cars. In contrast to the 911 Targa, it featured a narrow side window behind the door, and the C column was actually finished as the roll-over element. This bar slanted forward and divided the flank of the sports car from the large dome-like glass hatch. On some examples, the roll-over bar was clad in the same plastic material as the detachable centre section of the roof.

With some versions of the 924 Targa concepts, Porsche went even further. An internal description of 'test vehicle A13' from 1977 notes, among other things: 'The contour of the roof and rear window has been designed so that it is possible to slide a glass roof over the rear window.' However, this innovative idea was abandoned in spring 1980, as a perfect technical implementation was not yet possible. In fact, the 941/942 and A13 did not progress beyond the early prototype stage. Instead of a classic Targa, Porsche went on to offer the 924 with a large, removable roof made of plastic. Nonetheless, Porsche customers were soon calling this 924 a Targa. The idea of a sports car with a retractable glass roof disappeared into the filing cabinets at Weissach for another one and a half decades. It was finally resurrected and emerged in autumn 1995, in the form of the 911 Targa of the 993 model series.

__ It would have looked like this! Porsche developed very attractive Targa prototypes like this one for the 924. Even a glass roof sliding to the rear was considered.

# 51__935/80 Moby Dick 2

*A model athlete*

The 935/78 Moby Dick raced in 1978 and was a magnificent beast. Porsche's wizard of aerodynamics, Norbert Singer, had stretched this extreme 911 to a length of 4.89 metres with a long tail and a flat nose. At the same time, the white giant had grown in width and lost considerable height. Porsche's engine gurus developed a 3.2-litre, twin-turbo with up to 845 hp, and Moby Dick, weighing 1,025 kilos, reached a top speed of 366 kph at Le Mans.

Singer thought this was pretty good, but imagined something even better: greater driving stability, shorter braking distances, and above all higher cornering speeds. At this time, Formula 1 was experimenting with 'wing cars', whose sidepods, shaped like aircraft wings turned upside down, generated incredible downforce and allowed the single-seaters to zip through curves at lightning speed. Singer set out to investigate this 'ground effect' for what he would call the 'Moby Dick 2' using a 1:5-scale model. The diffuser at the rear end of the low pressure/high downforce zone under the car could not be positioned under the tail end due to the width of the flat-six engine. Norbert Singer, therefore, positioned the diffuser just behind the cockpit and in front of the turbo engine, allowing the air to exit at the lower end of the rear window. The wind tunnel was fired up, and the results of the first measurements looked promising. In comparison to the original Moby Dick, overall downforce rose by a massive 90 per cent. The balance of the downforce, too, gave grounds for optimism, as the low pressure also sucked the front end of the car to the track surface.

Nevertheless, Moby Dick 2 was never realised, remaining a 'model athlete' on a scale of 1:5. Porsche was charting a course towards the transaxle models and prototypes in motorsports. However, the idea still kept Singer occupied. The time finally came in 1982: the prototype 956, Porsche's first ground-effect racing car, took to the racetracks and proved to be an instant success.

___ The engineer Norbert Singer (left) and the author with the wind-tunnel model of Moby Dick 2. The downforce was huge, but Porsche's sports programme was heading in a different direction.

# 52_ Porsche 928 S4

*Racetrack and horse trailer*

Why would the prototype of a 928 S4 crawl up Mont Ventoux towing a heavily-laden trailer? Mont Ventoux, the famous hill-climb racecourse in Provence, 21.8 kilometres of winding roads from the little town of Bédoin up to the weather station, with a steep ascent of 1,612 metres.

The reason for this trip was a proposal by the bodywork development department (!) to replace the mechanically driven radiator fans of the five-litre V8 with electrically operated ones. The idea was that this would help to quench the 320 hp engine's thirst for fuel. A vehement head-shaking was the unanimous reaction from the engine specialists: impossible. Nevertheless, the bodywork team stuck to the idea, fitted two electric fans to the prototype and attached a trailer with the weight of two, shall we say, show-jumping horses, in it – after all, the 928 was often used to tow horse trailers. They then drove up Mont Ventoux.

The climb was a complete success. The engine temperatures remained healthy, and the 928 S4 went into series production with electric fans. Another masterstroke was the aerodynamics of the beautifully smoothed and rounded bodywork. In addition to many days in the wind tunnel, the at times quite rough and ready improvisation by Hermann Burst and his bodywork developers turned out to be fruitful. As Burst recalled in an interview in 2020: 'Heat tests were on the agenda in summer in Andalucía. The S4 was supposed to get aeroplates underneath and a modified aerokit. Our Herr Hochkönig had specialised in this subject, and he loved to experiment. On the way to Spain, Herr Hochkönig got us to stop at a scrapyard, he disappeared and then returned a little later with two armfuls of plastic canisters, cans and hoses. We trialled a wide variety of air ducting during our test drives using these materials. They turned out to be extremely helpful, and the designs were adopted for series production.'

The 928 S4 was significantly more streamlined than previous versions, with a top speed of 270 kph it ran faster than any other Porsche on the road, and thanks to the trailer as well as Mont Ventoux and the scrapyard, it consumed the same amount of fuel as its predecessor. A story worth knowing.

___ The 928 S4 on a test drive: heat tests in Andalucía and a hill climb up Mont Ventoux pulling a horse trailer lowered fuel consumption and raised the top speed.

# 53_Porsche 928 S4 Cabriolet Prototype H21

*Roaring and roofless*

Cruising with a view over an endlessly long bonnet and the sound of a large-capacity V8 in your ears can only be fully enjoyed under open skies. That's why when the 928 was conceived in the 1970s, a Targa version was initially regarded as a mouth-watering option. Obviously, it wasn't appetizing enough and it disappeared into oblivion. However, from the mid-1980s, the time seemed ripe for Porsche to add further variations of their 'big Gran Turismo' to the 928 Coupé. In addition to a study of a four-door, four-seater, Porsche's thought experiments resulted in a cabriolet with a fully retractable soft roof and a hardtop. The strategic planners at Porsche focused primarily on the healthy market on the west coast of the United States.

The basis of the roadster prototype dubbed H21 would be the 928 S4 with a five-litre, four-valve V8 engine that was good for 430 Newton-metres of torque at only 3,000 revs. 320 hp was enough to take the open-top 928 from zero to 100 kilometres per hour in about six seconds – despite an additional hundredweight compared to the coupé, a consequence of necessary chassis reinforcement. The gear diagram promised an entertaining maximum speed of 260 kph. Like its roofed cousins, the cabriolet provided every luxury that Porsche's programme offered at the time. For the safety of the passengers, high, robust headrests were installed, and the windscreen frame consisted of high tensile steel.

The Weinsberg bodywork plant of the American Sunroof Corporation (ASC), founded in 1965 in California by Heinz Prechter, built the drivable prototype in 1987 following Style Porsche designs. In the internal catalogue of the Porsche Museum in Stuttgart-Zuffenhausen, this cabriolet is called the 'USA Prechter adaptation'. Like the H50, its four-door, four-seat cousin, the H21, did not make it to series production, as the management board decided against the open-top version in the late 1980s. Two prototypes are said to have been made, one of which has survived in the Porsche Museum.

The prototype H21 was a Porsche 928 S4 with a fully retractable cabriolet roof and a 320 hp V8. Unfortunately, it did not eventuate, and only two prototypes were made.

# 54_ Porsche Indy P6B

*The goalposts moved*

By the end of the 1970s, Porsche was well on course to tackle the most important race in the USA: the 500 Miles of Indianapolis. In 1978, 400,000 spectators saw the race from the grandstands around the oval, and 60 million watched the drama on television.

The plan was as follows: Porsche would make the engine, while the Interscope team – run by the young and wealthy businessman Ted Field – would take care of the chassis. Both of these ingredients worked brilliantly. Porsche's engine guru Valentin Schäffer turned his attention to the racing engine of the 935/78 (based on the 911 engine!) with water-cooled cylinder heads and double turbocharging. He reduced the capacity to 2.65 litres, converted the six-cylinder boxer to run on methanol and with a single turbo, sacrificed a few piston rods and engine blocks on the testbed, to eventually end up with 906 hp at maximum boost. With the regulations permitting a pressure of 1.8 bars, 630 hp were possible according to Porsche. The chassis was the work of star designer Roman Slobodynskyj who had conceived several successful Indy cars. The lap times set by racing driver Danny Ongais during the first tests of the 680-kilo car on the Ontario Motor Speedway near Los Angeles raised eyebrows.

Four weeks before the start of the 1980 season, the United States Auto Club (USAC) informed Porsche's head of motorsports in the USA, Jo Hoppen, that the maximum boost for the six-cylinder engine would be reduced by two-tenths of a bar. Porsche abandoned the project. It was impossible to adapt the motor within a month. To this day there is speculation about what prompted the USAC to take this step. The laments of worried American teams or drivers threatening to quit if Porsche came in? Was it a late attempt to bring about a balance of performance? One welcome fact remains: Schäffer put five of his turbo engines aside when the Indy programme was halted. And when Porsche needed an engine for Le Mans in 1981, he pulled a petrol version out of his hat. It won and went on to power the 956 and 962C to legendary successes from 1982 onwards.

___ Ontario Speedway, 1979. The racing driver Danny Ongais next to the Porsche-powered Indy car. A combination that was fast from the very start but was never permitted to prove its potential.

PORSCHE
interscope
25
ONGAIS
DANNY ONGAIS
GOOD YEAR
Gabriel
SHELL
BOSCH
Arai

interscope
GOOD YEAR
25
25
interscope
PORS
GOODYEAR

— Chassis by the American team Interscope, engine by Porsche. The goal was to win the 500 Miles of Indianapolis in 1980. A last-minute change in the rules prevented Porsche's Indy P6B from competing.

# 55_Porsche 959 Aerodynamics Study C29

*Lofty artefact*

From time to time, the Porsche Museum in Stuttgart-Zuffenhausen rolls C29 out of the hangar, where seldom-seen Porsches rest, and into the exhibition. The orange and grey car standing there in a rather improvised fashion, covered with body-filler, sticky tape and hand-written scribbles is, in fact, an artefact from the very early development history of Porsche's super sportscar 959. C29 already existed in 1982 before the project officially began in January 1983.

Hermann Burst, born in 1940 and head of bodywork development at that time, recalled its genesis in spring 2020: 'Our R&D boss Helmuth Bott envisaged a sports car like nothing seen before, based on the 911, with a rear-engine, and with the proportions and lines of our 911.' The doors, boot lid, roof and B-column were to remain unchanged. The face, the rear end and the wings could be modified within limits. Burst and his team began experimenting with various versions of a 1:5-scale plasticine model in the wind tunnel of the Research Institute for Vehicles and Vehicle Engines (FKFS) in Stuttgart. Some of their work was intuitive, for example, the famous integrated rear wing. Burst and the modeller Michael Gallert created this first wing on a series-built Porsche fashioned from a piece of wood using a belt sander.

Helmuth Bott gave his enthusiastic blessing to the 1:5-model, and C29 was then made on a scale of 1:1. In contrast to Studio Style Porsche's 'Group B' concept car unveiled at the IAA motorshow in 1983, C29 not only had to look streamlined but also had to represent solutions for everyday motoring: enough ground clearance to drive into a garage, a healthy airflow through the radiator for the 450 hp, 2.8-litre, twin-turbo engine, cooling for the gearbox and the brakes – at top speed as well as in stop-and-go traffic of high summer. At the end of the work on C29, the drag coefficient was 0.31Cd, and – something only considered possible on a racing car – the 959 generated no lift when. A body shape had been found that was to become legendary.

___ The C29 in the wind tunnel showing clear signs of experimental craftsmanship. Calling on experience and intuition, the aerodynamics specialists often tried out dozens of solutions in a single day.

DNW
BB-P 732

The C29 aerodynamics study from 1982 – the creation of the bodywork for the Porsche 959 super sports car began with a lot of manual work in 1982.

# 56_ Porsche LMP 2000

*Hidden treasure*

'If a racing car runs well at the roll-out, then it's good. If it isn't fast at the roll-out, you have a tough job ahead of you,' says Allan McNish, a Scot born in 1969. McNish knows what he is talking about. He won Le Mans three times, was Endurance World Champion in 2013 and competed in Formula 1.

McNish recalls a cold, rainy November day in 1999 at the test track in Weissach. The new Le Mans prototype 900, dubbed internally as Type number 9R3 and popularly known as the LMP 2000, was about to undertake its first – and last – miles. It was an open racing car with a new 5.5-litre V10 normally aspirated engine that generated 615 hp with the mandatory restrictor. The carbon chassis was designed by Porsche and baked by Lola Composites. Norbert Singer conceived the innovative aerodynamics. The air from the front diffusers escaped laterally behind the front wheels, contributing significantly to the downforce on the front axle. Weighing 822 kgs, the car was still much too light. The regulations stipulated a weight of 900, and well-distributed ballast would be added later. McNish remembers: 'Bob Wollek and I had spent months testing components of the Spyder in the 911 GT1. Bob was the first to drive the LMP 2000, then it was my turn. The car was incredibly agile and the handling was nimble and precise. Under braking and in the curves, especially in the fast fourth-gear bend before the straight, I could feel the enormous, beautifully balanced downforce. The noisy engine had a superb throttle response. Better than our turbos. I only drove 30 kilometres, and a lot of things were still provisional, but I knew that this car could be a winner.'

'Could' was all that happened, as the project had already been stopped. The roll-out was not the beginning but the end. Other plans, such as developing the Cayenne, and the Carrera GT, took priority. Moreover, following the withdrawal of rivals for the 2000 season, there was no opposition in endurance motorsports. The 9R3, a secret, disappeared into a hangar. It was not until 2018 that the Spyder turned up again at the Festival of Speed in Goodwood, albeit just as a stationary exhibit. It looked fast and like a real winner, even when motionless.

___ The roll-out of the LMP 2000 on November 3, 1999. A mechanic holding a compressed-air starter crouches under the wing. Next to him stands works driver Allan McNish, in the cockpit sits racing driver Bob Wollek.

PORSCHE
Mobil 1
Mobil 1

# 57_ Porsche Cayenne S Jagdwagen

*Hunting, Porsche-style*

As a Porsche fan, you are probably familiar with the Type 597 Jagdwagen – a light, amphibious off-road vehicle. Porsche developed it in 1953–54 for the fledgling German army after an invitation to tender by the Ministry of Defence of the Federal Republic. But the Jagdwagen (or hunting car) featured here will probably be new to you.

The 2009 Jagdwagen was about style, or more precisely, hunting in Porsche-style. Porsche Tequipment played with this idea and converted a Cayenne S into a car for hunting parties. With four fog lamps on the roof and 19-inch all-terrain tyres, the prototype left no questions open: it was made for tough stuff. Inside, its 4.8-litre V8 was good for 385 hp and provided 500 Newton-metres of torque from 3,000 revs. Permanent four-wheel drive, a central differential lock, air suspension and a level control system made this 'hunting car' an almost unstoppable off-roader. The luggage compartment was home to an electric cable winch that could easily attach to the front bumper in 'sticky' situations. The boot housed a large steel pan to hold the quarry, and a large plastic tank next to it filled with water to clean the bounty of the hunt. The tool compartment under the pan provided generous space for all kinds of equipment, including an axe. An elegant metal-clad and lockable box for the weapons and ammunition lay across the back seats. The leather fittings in a sand-beige colour exuded the aura of a luxurious hunting lodge on wheels.

Concepts for possible special editions and exclusive models are constantly created at Porsche in order to explore market interests. Their number is the well-hidden secret of a select few at Zuffenhausen and Weissach. Only a handful of those prototypes make it to production. The hunting car did not, it remained a one-off that is occasionally put on display at the Porsche Museum in Stuttgart-Zuffenhausen.

__ The 2009 Cayenne S Jagdwagen appeared somewhat martial and offered functionality for modern-day hunters plus a dash of luxury thanks to the fine leather trim of the interior.

HELLA
HELLA
HELLA
HELLA
PORSCHE
MUSEUM
JAGDWAGEN
BFGoodrich
All-Terrain T/A

# 58_ Porsche Boxster Bergspyder

*Return to adventure*

In 1968, Porsche created the 909 Bergspyder, an extreme racing car for the European Hillclimb Championship. This mighty midget weighed a mere 384 kilos, rapidly propelled by a 275 hp, eight-cylinder engine. In 2015, a team of engineers in Weissach chose the word 'Bergspyder' ('mountain Spyder') as the motto in developing a Boxster prototype. The question was: 'How light can we make a 981? How far can we pare the sports car down to one thing: driving?'

The result of their work was a one-off vehicle, a single-seater embodying the most delicious features from Porsche racing history. There was the flat, semi-circular windbreak in front of the driver at shoulder height, and the rear-view mirror on a stalk reminiscent of those that adorned almost all of the early Spyders. The cockpit cover next to the driver already existed on the 356 Speedster and 550 Spyder in 1954, however, for the 2015 Bergspyder it was made of artificial leather instead of aluminium. Just like in the early racing days of the 356 and the 909 Bergspyder, door handles were dispensed with.

Alongside all the history, the 981 Bergspyder had a great deal of contemporary Porsche elements on board. The bonnet and engine lid were made of carbon fibre, as was the seat, which the Weissach engineers borrowed from the 918 Spyder super-sports car. In contrast to its eponymous predecessor, the 2015 vintage Bergspyder even manifested traces of everyday functionality. In addition to the luggage space in the front, there was another baggage compartment and space for the helmet in place of the passenger seat. The heart of this mid-engine sports machine came from the Cayman GT4, a six-cylinder flat engine that generated 393 hp from 3.8 litres. This was enough to catapult the 1,099-kilogram single-seater to 100 kilometres per hour in just under four seconds. So far, so brilliant. But, according to Porsche, the Boxster Bergspyder did not make it beyond the prototype stage as certain countries would have baulked at giving this swashbuckling machine road homologation.

__ A radically reduced driving machine in 2015. With plenty of carbon fibre, minimal fittings and no roof, the Boxster Bergspyder weighed in at 1,099 kilograms.

Porsche Museum

Three Porsche 904 Carrera GTSs parked at the Werk 2 in Zuffenhausen in 1964, surrounded by a number of 356s. A car park full of legends, the origins of which this chapter will explore.

# CARS & A CREST

# 59_Porsche 356

*The first one from Stuttgart*

Porsche was forced to leave bomb-raided Stuttgart in 1944. The first 356 was put on its wheels in Gmünd, Austria, in 1948, with a small production run of 52 356/2s to follow. However, the future of the ambitious car manufacturer did not lie in the beautiful, remote Austrian province of Carinthia. Before it was possible to return to Stuttgart, where Ferdinand Porsche had opened his first design office in 1931, a number of serendipitous events had to align.

They did. Ferry Porsche successfully negotiated a solid financial basis with Volkswagen. For every Beetle that was built from September 1949, Porsche received a licence fee. After all, the best-seller was a Porsche design. But Porsche also needed a factory. The US Army occupied the old factory in Zuffenhausen where the GIs repaired their Jeeps. Porsche's family villa with its small workshop was certainly not an option. However, opposite the old Porsche site in Stuttgart, the Karosseriewerk Reutter ran one of its bodywork plants. Reutter had been a partner since the 1930s. The coachwork company leased a 600-square-metre hall to Porsche for the production of the four cylinders and the transmissions. Porsche and Reutter concluded their agreement without any paperwork – a handshake sufficed. The bodywork and interiors were made at Reutter's major plant in the west of Stuttgart, and the marriage of the bodywork, chassis and power train was celebrated in the Porsche factory hall.

Production began in March 1950. Porsche employees pushed the first 356 out of the small hall in Zuffenhausen on April 6, 1950. It was a coupé with the chassis number 5002. Thus, the 15-year success story of the 356 began with 1,086 cc and 40 horsepower, a four-speed gearbox from Volkswagen, drum brakes, torsion spring suspension, acceleration from zero to 100 kph in 23.5 seconds and a top speed of 140 kph. A dream sports car indeed, and the first chapter of a success story. Series production in Zuffenhausen ended on 28 April, 1965. In May 1966, the Dutch motorway police took delivery of the last ten 356 Cs, and the story concluded after the last of 77,766 units rolled off the assembly line.

— This is the first Porsche 356 produced in Stuttgart, photographed on April 6, 1950. The paintwork is light grey, and the hub caps are taken from the Beetle. All in all, a dream sports car.

PORSCHE
AW 21-0459

0459

Another image of the first Stuttgart-made 356. The workers gave nicknames to special cars. This one was the 'Greyhound'.

# 60_ Porsche 356 A 1500 GS Carrera

*How 'Carrera' hit the road*

It is a well-known story: Hans Herrmann drove a 550 1500 RS Spyder in the 1954 Carrera Panamericana over 3,000 kilometres from the south to the north of Mexico. Herrmann left most of his competitors with significantly brawnier engines in his dust and clinched third overall with the tiny Porsche. Herrmann's Porsche was powered by a new 1.5-litre engine that put out 110 hp in the racing version. Ernst Fuhrmann had designed this complicated four-cylinder motor with vertical shafts driving two camshafts per cylinder head in 1953. The Type 547 flat was an intricate three-dimensional mosaic.

The year after victory in Mexico, Porsche presented the second generation of the 356 made in Zuffenhausen: the 356 A. Under the rear lid of the top version growled a 100-hp variant of the 'Fuhrmann engine'. Its origins were undeniable. Conceived for racing, the engine responded rather tepidly to hesitancy on the throttle pedal. To feel at its best, the light-metal unit needed revs and more revs, and then it communicated pure joy, a beautiful sound and an impressive punch. It maxed out at 6,200 revs, the sprint to 100 kph took only twelve seconds, and top speed was just under 200 kph. With aluminium lids and doors, this top 356 A weighed a mere 820 kilos. Inside, the fastest road-legal Porsche displayed its temperament with a rev counter that went up to 8,000, a speedometer with a scale reaching 250 kph, and sporty bucket seats.

A fiery temperament like this needed a name. Since the episode in Mexico, the word 'Carrera' had often been bandied about in connection with Ernst Fuhrmann's engine. And, from 1955, the 356 A 1500 GS Carrera was the first sports car from Zuffenhausen to bear the Spanish word for 'race' in its name. For many years, 'Carrera' was reserved for the most powerful vehicles and the racing versions of Porsche's model families. Porsche built only 447 units of the first Carrera, in coupé, cabriolet and Speedster versions. The first Carreras to grace Porsche dealerships back then came with a hefty 18,500 Deutschmarks price tag. Today, those classics easily command six-figure sums at auctions.

__ A 356 A 1500 Grand Sport Carrera in action at the Badischer Bäderpreis competition in 1956. The Carrera lettering can just be seen in front of the door.

S 33·400

A stylish way to buy fruit – through the roof of the 100 hp Porsche 356 A 1500 GS Carrera, which Porsche sold from 1955.

S 199

# 61_The Porsche Crest

*It all started with Dr Domnick*

Dr Ottomar Domnick, a neurologist and lover of art, collected his fish-silver 356 from Zuffenhausen on May 26, 1950. Ferry Porsche referred to the good doctor as 'the first customer'. It is well documented that the chassis number of his Porsche was 5005 and that Domnick lamented the absence of a crest on the coupé.

To remedy this oversight, he proposed a competition to find a logo, which Porsche held in 1951 under the name 'Porsche Prize'. The foreword to the brochure for the Porsche Prize states: 'It is in the spirit of Dr Ferdinand Porsche to set young people a task of great responsibility. To this end, Porsche KG, Stuttgart, has decided to hold a competition for the design of their company logo and address it to art academies. May the academies [...] be aware of their responsibility to serve the everyday work of industry.' Ten academies submitted numerous designs – but none of them convinced Porsche.

So, Ferry Porsche travelled to New York around the same time to talk business with the major importer Max Hoffman. Hoffman knew what his customers wanted. The confidential report by Porsche's assistant Ghislaine Kaes dated December 27, 1951, records that: 'Mr Hoffman regards a plaque on the dashboard with "Porsche" and the Stuttgart coat of arms on it as being a far from insignificant sales factor.' More specifically, Hoffman wished to see 'the steering-wheel hub decorated with "Porsche" and the coat of arms of Stuttgart or something similar.'

For lack of suitable proposals, Ferry Porsche and his designer Franz Xaver Reimspiess took up their pens in 1952. Reimspiess had designed not only the Beetle engine but also the logo with a 'V' and a 'W' in a circle: Volkswagen. Porsche and Reimspiess combined the famous Porsche lettering with a prancing horse and the arms of the state of Württemberg. It first appeared on the horn buttons in 1952 and on the bonnet handle of the 356 in 1954. Today, the horse theme is delightfully incorporated in the Taycan's name. The name of Porsche's first fully electric sports car means a "young, prancing horse."

— Some of the very first customers bemoaned the lack of a crest on sports cars from Zuffenhausen. The badge has adorned the horn buttons of Porsches since 1952.

PORSCHE

# 62_ Porsche 356 C 1600 SC Police Cabriolet

*Open-air from five degrees*

The first Porsche 356 featured a canvas top. And for all the following generations of this classic car from the 356/2 to the 356, A, B and C, Porsche supplied soft-top versions, which were all beautiful and all more expensive than their coupé cousins.

For a few lucky people, the cabriolet became a workplace on wheels. In 1964, Porsche 356 C 1600 SC Cabriolets patrolled the highways of the federal state of Baden-Württemberg, using the most powerful pushrod engine that Porsche planted in a 356 at the time. The four-cylinder flat motor produced 95 hp from 1,582 cc. It goes without saying that the sports engine needed lively revs. Below 2,500 not much happened. Above, however, progress was vigorous up to 5,500 revs. The 1600 SC reached 100 kph in 11.5 seconds, with its top speed at 185 kilometres per hour. Disc brakes all round ensured the necessary deceleration in case motorised villains attempted to escape via the twisty roads of the Black Forest. With a blue flashing light, a siren, a radio, a fire extinguisher, special tools and a large fuel tank (from the GT models), the police Porsche was well equipped for the job.

Whenever the Autobahnpolizei needed new recruits for the cockpits of their Porsches, hundreds of candidates applied. As it took quite some skill to drive a 356 fast, the newly chosen Porsche police officers completed a driving training at Weissach. The prestigious job in the cabriolet did have its downside, however. According to duty regulations, the car had to be driven with the roof open at temperatures above five degrees Celsius. And the crew's egg-shaped safety helmets were not exactly a fashion statement.

The story of Porsche police cars did not begin with the last generation of the 356. From the mid-1950s, in several European countries, members of the police force had the pleasure of delivering high-speed services to the nation in sports cars from Zuffenhausen. The story of the 356 in police service ended in May 1966, when Porsche delivered the last ten 356 C cabriolets to the Rijkspolitie in the Netherlands.

__ These policemen maintained an impression of solemnity, but inside they must have been jumping for joy. The Porsche cabriolet was a greatly coveted workplace.

PORSCHE
AW 24-8919

A sports car that most people didn't dare to even dream of in post-war Germany. The 356 Cabriolet, with a 1.3-litre engine, cost 13,400 Deutschmarks in 1954, about as much as three standard Beetles.

# 63_ Porsche 904 Carrera GTS

*Racing beauty*

Porsche unveiled the 904 Carrera Gran Turismo Sport on November 26, 1963, at the Solitude racetrack in Stuttgart. The mid-engine two-seater was a beauty, and an extremely versatile sports car. Porsche made 106 examples of the sports car powered by a 155 hp, two-litre vertical shaft motor. Thanks to a sports exhaust, 180 hp at 7,200 revs made it possible to go racing at weekends. For the five-speed gearbox, Porsche supplied different gearings with the names Nürburgring, hillclimb, airfield racing and Le Mans. The double wishbones, anti-roll bars and hydraulic brakes were among the finest items that Porsche had on stock in Zuffenhausen. Customers raced the 650-kilo lightweight with great success all around the world.

The works team also placed its trust in the four-cylinder engine initially and won the Targa Florio straight off the bat in 1964. The 904 scooped the first four positions in its class at Le Mans and demonstrated its all-round talent by taking second place in deep snow at the 1965 Monte Carlo Rally. The Monte Carlo contender already sported the new 210 hp, two-litre, six-cylinder Type 901 from the 911. For the factory team, Porsche even planted the Type 771, two-litre, eight-cylinder unit with 240 hp into two of their 904 Carrera GTS. Only the factory entered the six-cylinder and eight-cylinder versions, winning the two-litre GT class of the International Manufacturers Championship in 1964 and 1965.

It is, however, the unique bodywork design by F. A. Porsche that makes the Carrera GTS an epoch-making Zuffenhausen sports car. To this day, the 904 is regarded as one of the most beautiful designs on four wheels. And it marks the beginning of plastic bodywork at Porsche. To save money, the company had the outer shell made of fibreglass at the Henkel aircraft plant based at the German city of Speyer. The process was still in its infancy, which sometimes resulted in irregularities and uneven thicknesses of the material, thus explaining the bodyweight of up to a hundred kilos. The racing mechanics of the day did not necessarily see this as a disadvantage. As one of the men recalls: 'You could even get a screw into the plastic. And it stayed in.'

__ A very early 904 Carrera GTS at the Porsche Werk 2, 1963. The mid-engine car designed by F. A. Porsche is still considered one of the most beautiful sports vehicles ever.

— Mid-mounted engine, plastic bodywork: the Porsche 904 Carrera GTS driven by Schiller and Siffert in the Nürburgring 1,000 km race in May 1964.

65
team
SCHILLER
65

# 64_ 911 Targa

*Money saved, legend born*

The Porsche 901 Coupé was ready to be launched in 1963, but the folk at Zuffenhausen had a bit of a headache: how can we create an 'open 901' without completely exhausting funds that were already depleted by the development of our coupé? A cabriolet meant increasing the rigidity of the bodywork, a new rear to accommodate the folding top and expensive new tools for its production.

That was too much. Moreover, reports from the USA led to fears of a ban on open automobiles of the 356 Speedster and cabrio ilk. Was a roll-over bar the solution, like in racing cars? There were proposals on the table, and once the designers transformed the plain steel pipes into a handsome bar, clad in brushed steel, the solution was found.

Porsche had the 'safety cabriolet' patented in August 1965. Now a catchy name was needed for this fresh-air sports car. Porsche's top managers sat down and brainstormed. They soon hit upon the idea of using racetrack names. Finally, the head of sales, Harald Wagner, came up with the magic word: 'Targa'. The Targa Florio was a road race in Sicily that Porsche had won five times by 1964. Only hard-core racing fans would have understood 'Florio', and others would have associated the term with a flower shop. So there it is: 'Targa'. It sounded exotic, suggested speed, and perhaps even evoked images of Sicilian coastal roads? Just as the word 'Carrera' had lent its exotic aura for ten years, first to an engine, and then to special Porsche sports cars.

At the 1965 IAA automobile show in Frankfurt, fans and the media were delighted by the 911 Targa. The German Autobahnpolizei were the first to enjoy the open-top 911, using it from December 1966. The Targa went on sale in January 1967 and was an immediate success. Since then, Porsche has created a Targa for all eight generations of the 911 – sometimes classical, sometimes with a glass roof, sometimes with a sophisticated cinematic surpassed only by transformers… but always fascinating.

__ A pre-production 911 2.0 Targa from 1965. The plastic rear window became known as the soft window. It could be unzipped and removed, and at times proved a challenge to operate.

An early Porsche 911 Targa airborne on the Volkswagen test track near Wolfsburg in the 1960s.

# 65_Porsche 917-001

*A passion for 001*

The 917 is Porsche's most famous racing car. 917-001 was the first of this wild species, and at the Geneva Auto Show on March 12, 1969, it made jaws drop. Then 001 went on tour for presentations, briefly ran tests at Weissach, and in autumn 1970, Porsche presented it as a showcar in the red-and-white livery and the short-tail body of their first Le Mans winner (which was, in fact, chassis number 023).

In 2017, Porsche decided to restore 001 to its original condition and entrusted the mission to Armin Burger as the motorsports coordinator of the Porsche Museum. Burger first talked to the people who were involved back in the day: How did you build it? What is still original on the car? The critical moment of disassembling the vehicle arrived in February 2018. The four-man restoration team felt on edge – after all, it's not every day that you dissect a monument. To everyone's relief, much of 001 had survived, including the aluminium space frame, albeit without the long-tail section of the original. The roof, the doors, the window frames, engine, gearbox and chassis were still there. Even the cavities in the fuel tanks and the oil reservoir for the original side pipes came to light. There were many reminders of 001's long life: when stripped back, the pale blue Gulf paintwork from the presentation in London in October 1969 reappeared. The steering wheel and the switches still had the old sheen. Features that had been lost were made anew by special companies: the long-tail body part, recreated with the help of old drawings and laminating plans, the toned Plexiglas window above the engine, the cast magnesium wheels. The movable spoiler flaps at the rear posed a delicate challenge. As Burger said: 'There were no longer any drawings. We reconstructed the flaps from old pictures. They work perfectly, and now we have drawings again.'

In March 2019, 917-001 was finally restored to how it looked 50 years before in Geneva – an example of the huge passion of Porsche people like Burger. When asked about the year of his birth, Burger replied to the author: '1970. The year Porsche won Le Mans for the first time.'

___ The proud crew with 917-001 after its restoration in the workshop. Armin Burger stands on the far left. If you look closely, you may recognise many prominent Porsche people.

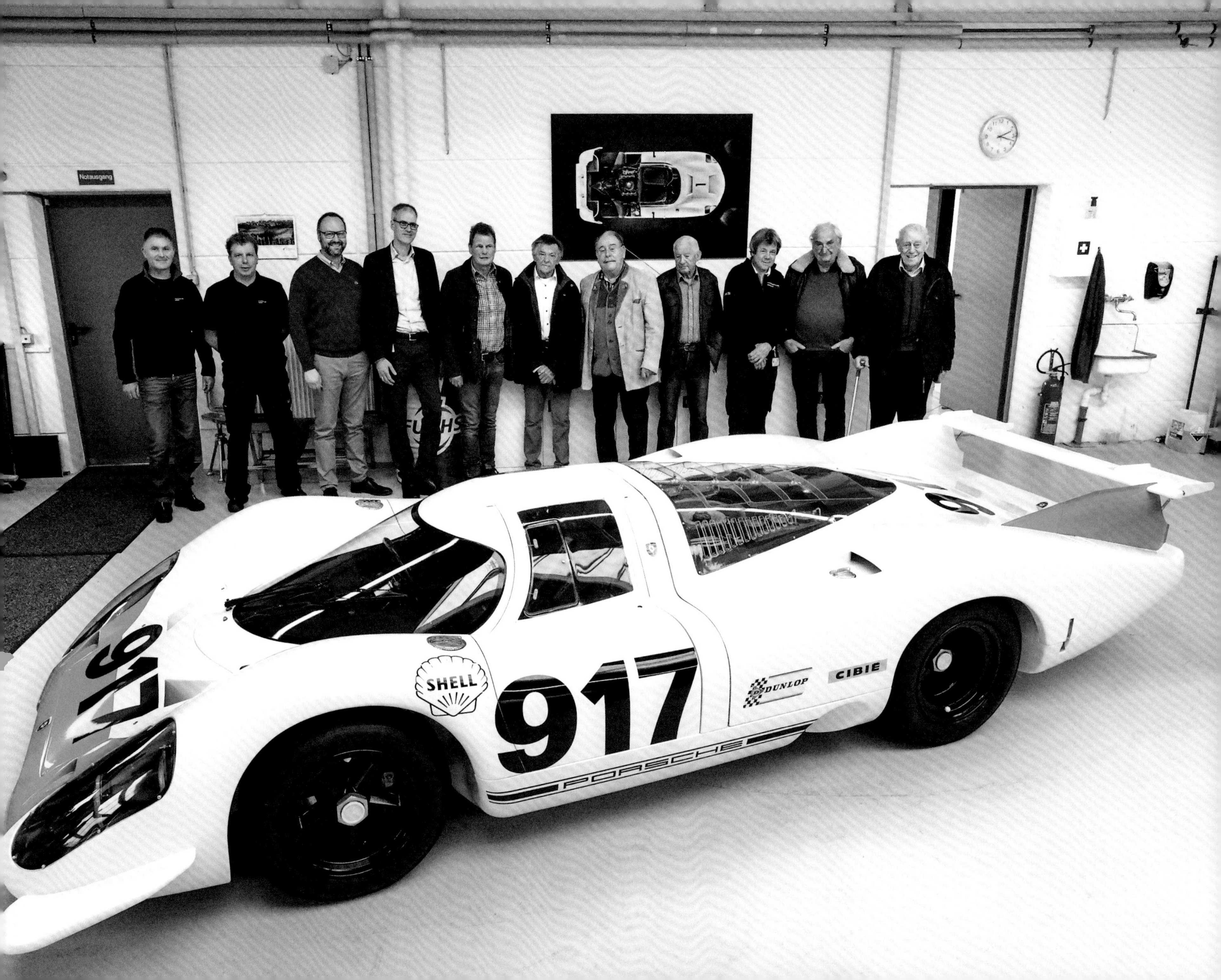
Notausgang
SHELL
917
DUNLOP
CIBIE
PORSCHE

# 66_ Porsche 911 GT2

*Wild thing!*

Porsche's fastest, most powerful and most expensive 911s with road homologation have displayed the GT2 badge on the engine lid since 1995. They are all derived from the 911 Turbo. They feature rear-wheel-drive, are rare and come with racing genes.

The first Porsche 911 GT2 looked as if it had just rolled off the test track with its screwed-on plastic wing extensions, a bulky front spoiler and a large wing at the rear. At low speeds, the adjustable sports suspension made the GT2 jerk stiffly in the way that only racing cars do. 430 hp, and later 450 hp from the 3.6-litre, twin-turbo engine, combined with a classic lightweight design, made for a power-to-weight ratio of three kilos per hp. The dash to 100 kph was over after a little less than four seconds; maximum speed was reached at 295 kph. By 1997, Porsche had produced 193 units of the road racer and happily handed out the ignition key to the enthusiastic new owner in exchange for a little more than 290,000 Deutschmarks.

The next generations of Porsche's 'wild thing' became more powerful and faster until reaching a pinnacle in 2017. A 3.8-litre, twin-turbo engine producing 700 hp provides decent thrust for the GT2 RS Type 991. According to Porsche, one horsepower moves just 2.1 kilos. Porsche made generous use of carbon-fibre with the front and rear lids and rear wing, while the roof is made of magnesium and the exhaust system of titanium. The 991 GT2 RS accelerates from zero to 100 kph in 2.8 seconds, and 8.3 seconds are enough to break the 200 barrier. Top speed is 340 kph. In October 2018, the GT2 RS – equipped with refinements such as four-wheel steering and dynamic engine bearings ex-works – gave an impressive demonstration of its dynamic capabilities on the Nürburgring Nordschleife, setting a record lap of just under 6:40 minutes. And the wildest 911 went on to turn fastest laps around legendary American racetracks such as Road America and Road Atlanta.

About four weeks after the scheduled end of production in February 2019, a cargo ship with four GT2 RS destined for Brazil (basic price: 285,220 euros) on board sank in the Atlantic. As very loyal customers were waiting for their new Nine-Elevens in South America, Porsche built another four GT2 RS. Now that's customer service!

___ The road version of the first 911 GT2 at a presentation in spring 1995 (recognise the driver?). It began here with 430 hp, whereas the latest GT2 RS generates 700 horsepower.

S-LZ 4088

1

An example of the first 911 GT2 generation is taken through its paces on a circuit. Porsche offered this 430 hp car with a top speed of 295 kph as a basis for racing cars from 1995.

# 67__Porsche Boxster Spyder

*'More smiles per gallon'*

Perfection can be a source of joy. So can small everyday adventures: a drive in the 2010 Boxster Spyder for example. Dark clouds, lightning, a shower of rain on the horizon. No roof over your head and no sign of a bridge to take shelter under. Stop the car, jump out, retrieve the soft roof and the rolled-up rear window from the storage above the engine. Fix them in position by hand the right way round, fasten the canvas properly. With a lot of practice, this can be done in two or three minutes, and it is fun to fumble against the clock, leaping into the cockpit seconds before the first heavy drops pound on the fabric roof. This does not, however, mean that the two in the cockpit stay dry. Even at moderate speeds, a gap opens above the side windows, and, according to Porsche, more than 200 kph is not advisable with this wonderfully rudimentary overhead protection in place. Cleaning the Spyder in a carwash? Forget it!

The Spyder is about driving, not washing. Without the roof and with 320 hp at hand, Porsche promises a top speed of 267 kilometres per hour. That is if you are ready for a hurricane to roar around your head. With an official kerb weight of 1,275 kilograms, the Spyder was the lightest Porsche with road-traffic approval in its day. The mid-engine beast sprinted from zero to 100 kph in just 5.1 seconds and fulfilled every sports car promise thanks to a stiff sports suspension and 19-inch rims fitted with some impressive rubber. The manual six-speed gearbox, the painted metal central console and the rear spoiler attached like the duck tail intensify the impression of traditional manufacturing craftsmanship. A hardtop and a seven-speed PDK gearbox were available as extras. But who would have opted for those? Back to the roots was the motto, back to no-frills sporty driving. Those who were happy with the price of the most expensive Boxster of its time, and who were not afraid of the occasional outdoor shower, reaped rich rewards. A Californian fan described it like this: 'In the Boxster Spyder you simply get more smiles per gallon.'

__ Back to the roots of sporty no-frills driving was the motto. This Spyder was the most expensive Boxster in its day with the most minimal roof ever.

PORSCHE

# 68 Porsche Tractor

*Not your usual Porsche*

Back in 1946, Porsche's head designer Karl Rabe penned plans for a diesel tractor, and in 1950 the company Allgaier Maschinenbau, based in Uhingen near Stuttgart, began production under the licence of the "System Porsche" Allgaier tractor. In Uhingen and at the factory in Manzell near Friedrichshafen on Lake Constance, Allgaier made low-cost, versatile tractors with one- to four-cylinder engines. They boasted such technical treats as an oil-hydraulic clutch for getting underway without jolts and stutters.

After more than 25,000 Allgaier tractors had been made, Mannesmann AG paid millions to take over the licence and the production facility on Lake Constance in late 1955. From this point on, the tractors were manufactured by 'Porsche-Diesel Motorenbau'. Zuffenhausen continued to supply the air-cooled engines, as well as many of the accessories and bright ideas such as 'HydroStop', by which the tractor could be controlled and steered remotely with an extension of the fluid coupler. Typically for Porsche, the red (or occasionally 'traffic orange') tractors with beige-coloured wheels looked handsome. The nose-shaped engine cover was a design gimmick that, although impractical, lent a touch of dynamism even to this Porsche.

In the late 1950s and early 1960s, the Porsche tractors stormed (well, let's say 'dieseled') to the top of German sales statistics. The lighter Junior and Standard models were especially sought-after by owners of smaller farms. On huge estates in North and South America or in Africa, Porsche tractors hardly cut the mustard. The power seemed too low at a maximum of 50 hp, and the prices for accessories that competitors provided in a package were too high. Germany also lacked contacts to overseas countries, where competitors sold subsidised tractors, for example, through established sales channels in the British Commonwealth. Nevertheless, some 100,000 tractors were made in seven years by Porsche-Diesel Motorenbau. When the last 'red-nose' left the assembly line in 1963, Porsche tractor fans around the globe had already fallen in love with the slow vehicles bearing the fast name.

A Standard model circa 1960. 'HydroStop' allowed the remote control of attached machinery or even the steering of the tractor while walking beside it.

Some words emanate magic, and there are places that represent entire histories. Here is a small selection.

# WORDS & PLACES

Oberflächenbehandlung bei Vergoldung:

Untersilberung = 4 μ
Vergoldung = 3 μ

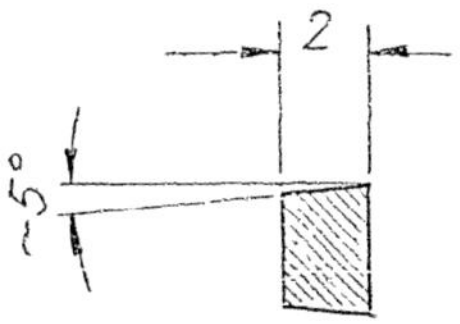


Schnitt A-A
M.5:1

Oberfläche glanz-vergoldet
Fasen – matt vergoldet
Rückseite grundiert od. samtiert – mit Kunstseideflocken.

Wenn kein Abmaß angegeben, gilt



Dr. Ing. h. c. F. Porsche K.-G.
Stuttgart-Zuffenhausen, den

| | Gezeichnet | Geprüft | Normgeprüft | Gesehen | Maßstab |
|---|---|---|---|---|---|
| Tag | 10.9.54 | | | | 1:1 |
| Name | Franck. | | | | 5:1 |

| | |
|---|---|
| Rohgew. je 1 Stck. kg | Ersatz für |
| Fertiggew. je 1 Stck. kg | Ersetzt durch |

| Nr. | Änderung | Tag | Name | Gepr. |
|---|---|---|---|---|

Werkstoff u. Rohmaße: Bronze- od. Messingblech, -Guß vergoldet – verniert

Ben.: Schriftzug „Spyder"

Stück | Z. Nr. 550.58.350

# 69_ Porsche Design

*Superyacht, grand piano, tobacco pipe*

Flugplatzstrasse 29, in Zell am See, 40 miles south of Salzburg: this is the address of Studio F. A. Porsche, the creative heart of the Porsche Design Group. A wholly-owned subsidiary of Porsche AG since 2017, the studio with its 30 employees is responsible for all products of the exclusive lifestyle brand Porsche Design and for the design of the Porsche Driver's Selection. Items with the discreet 'pd' logo combine clean and timeless design with the finest quality – at corresponding prices. Studio F. A. Porsche also creates product, transport and spatial designs, as well as brand strategies on commission. The group is the wellspring of designs for superyachts, cable-car cabins, furnishings for private jets and occasionally such items as a grand piano for the manufacturer Bösendorfer (lightweight honeycomb lid with a gas pressured spring).

The origins of the Porsche Design Group and thus Studio F. A. Porsche go back to 1972 when the Porsche family withdrew from key managerial positions in the company. Ferdinand Alexander Porsche, the head designer, founded Porsche Design in the same year and relocated it from Stuttgart to Zell am See in 1974. 'F. A.' had spent his childhood years there on the Schüttgut, the family estate.

The first commission in 1972 was a wristwatch for employees celebrating their anniversary at Porsche with a guaranteed purchase of 20 per annum. F. A. Porsche designed according to his core beliefs: 'Optimise the function, reduce the form uncompromisingly to essentials. Go above and beyond the familiar to continually discover new, better solutions.' The result is the legendary Chronograph 1, a matt-black automatic timepiece conceived in an era of euphoria for quartz and digital watches. Chrono 1 set standards and remains a style-defining product to this day. Another frequently mentioned piece by F. A. Porsche was his wooden pipe made from briar root. Cooling gills around the bowl of the pipe keep the combustion temperature of the tobacco low, preventing the finer nuances of taste from being scorched. A different take on air-cooling, but typical of Porsche.

___ F. A. Porsche at Zell am See, July 2003. First, he conceived the shape of the 911, then he founded Porsche Design.

PORSCHE DESIGN
S GO 90
MN-P 911
ZE 72 PG

# 70_ Porsche Museum, Zuffenhausen

*A journey back in time*

From 1976, the Porsche Museum at Porschestrasse No. 42 in Zuffenhausen exhibited about 20 sports and racing cars in a small hall. In 2005, work began on a building more befitting the exclusive image of the sports car brand on the nearby Porscheplatz. Today, the futuristic structure towers over the square, resembling a giant UFO that has just landed on a friendly mission. Thanks to 6,000 tonnes of invisibly incorporated steel framework, the large, transparent façade seems to hover high above the ground. Up there, the expansive glass façade allows glimpses of sports cars, racing cars, and engines. For those with a weakness for hedonistic motoring, this sight has the same effect as the display window of a delicatessen has on a gourmet.

The glass doors first opened on January 31, 2009, and by summer 2019, 4.7 million visitors had passed through them to take a journey back in time. Behind a glass wall in the foyer, the museum's specialists restore historic Porsches from the museum collection in full view of the public. Guided tours of the museum and factory start here, and here you'll find one of the two museum restaurants, not to forget the irresistible shop. From the ground floor, visitors can take the escalator or elevators to an exhibition space that spreads across some 5,600 square metres. The museum offers a changing display of 90 Porsches at a time, accompanied by films, texts and models. All in all, the museum holds a collection of 700 cars. The interior of the UFO offers spacious areas for concerts, readings and events alongside the exhibitions. For the 'Porsche Sound Night', the museum invites fans to Stuttgart's Porsche Arena, where a few thousand aficionados listen to the symphonies of Porsche engines on stage.

While the museum is located at the Porscheplatz in Stuttgart, its cars are constantly on the move. In 2019, motoring delicacies from Zuffenhausen were showcased at 270 events all around the world. For the second decade of the 21st century, the museum is on their 'Mission Future Heritage', following the credo that there is no future without an origin.

___ A 910/8 Bergspyder in the workshop of the Porsche Museum. Historic Porsches from the collection are restored here in full view of visitors.

Quaker State
PORSCHE
1

PORSCHE
F.A.T.
INTERNATIONAL
GROUPAGES EUROPÉENS
35
F.A.T.
INTERNATIONAL
GROUPAGES EUROPÉENS

With a little luck, such rarities as this Porsche 962 Dauer LM GT can be found in the parking lot of the Porsche Museum. This car contested just one race: Le Mans in 1994.

# 71_Air-Cooled

*Cool to the core*

Porsche 'air-cooled' stands for plain, gnarly, authentic. Craftsmanship with tradition. And nostalgia. 'Air-cooled' builds the bridge back to the early days of Porsches, with the four-cylinder boxer engine of the 356. Then came the first four generations of the 911 powered by flat-sixes and a sound between a rattle and a grizzly roar, not muzzled by a mantle of cooling water. 'Air-cooled' evokes memories of empty country roads and of the days when the village policeman was a race fan. Besides, in the words of a Volkswagen slogan: 'Air does not boil, air does not freeze.' One could add, with lightweight construction in mind, that a litre of air weighs about 1.3 grams, while a litre of water weighs a kilo.

'Air-cooled', as a sign of the origin, quality and character of Porsche sports cars, seems to have been born and nurtured primarily in the hearts of enthusiasts rather than in the heads of the engineers at Zuffenhausen and Weissach.

Porsche stayed true to air cooling in motor racing for a long time, possibly to prove, as a boost to the Volkswagen image, that air-cooled also means power. However, in spite of 1,100 turbo hp from the 5.4-litre twin-turbo of the 917/30 in 1973, it became clear that there was no way around water for a higher output per litre. First around the cylinder heads (1978), then in the entire engine (1985).

On the road, the 959 ran with water-cooled heads from 1988. Ten years later, in March 1998, Porsche produced the last air-cooled engine for a 911. The engineering challenge of making an air-cooled engine fit for modern noise and exhaust requirements had become too complex – and expensive.

The curtain fell on the affair, but the love lasted and now blossoms beautifully among communities of fans, such as the one started by the American Porsche works racing driver Patrick Long and his buddy, the star designer Howie Idelson. Their spectacular and creative 'Luftgekühlt' meets have been 'the coolest show on earth' for fans of classic Porsches since 2014.

___ A legendary air-cooled engine: the eight-cylinder Type 771 produced a massive 272 hp from 1,981 cc in 1967. But ultimately, there was no way around water-cooling, both on the road and the racetrack.

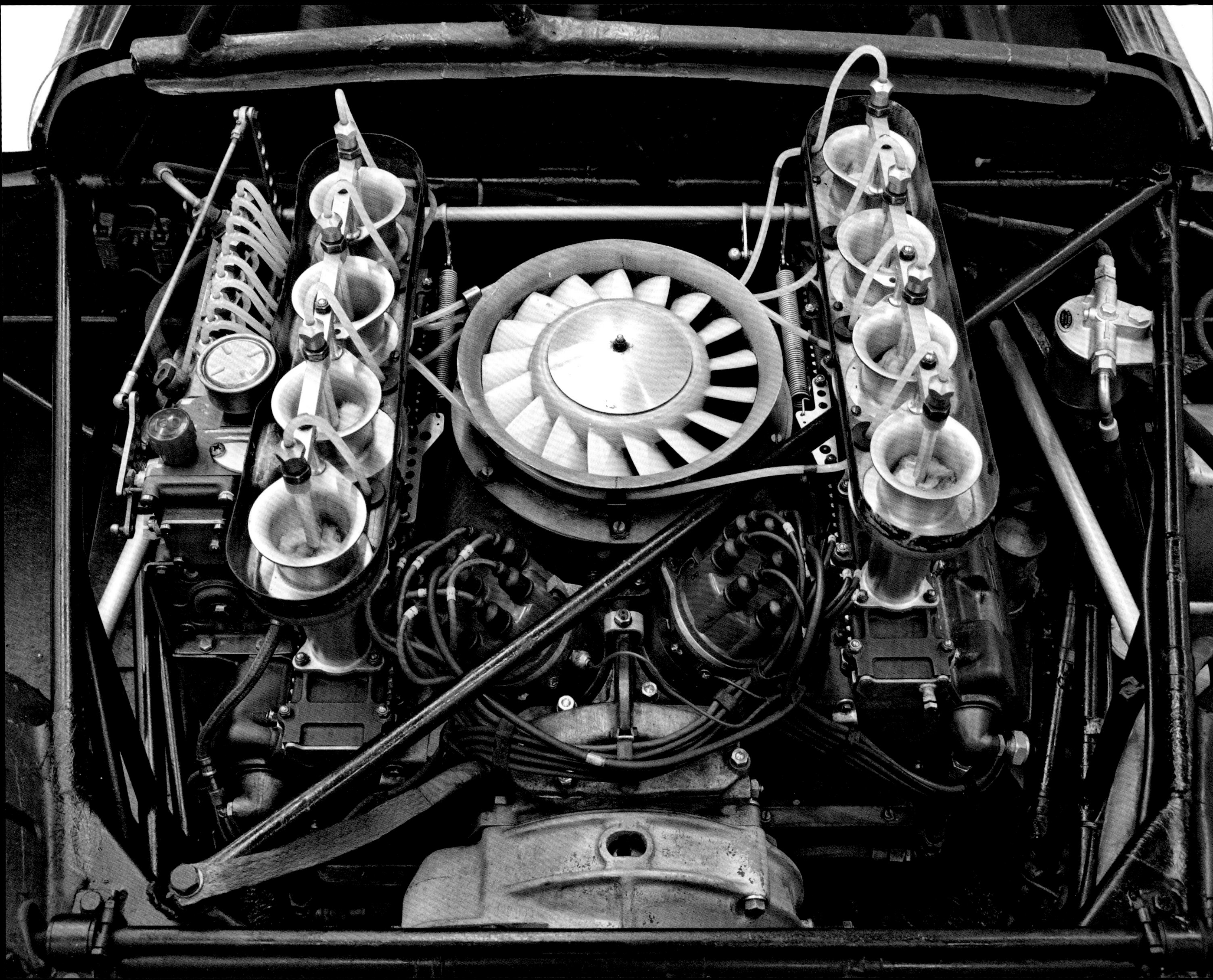

# 72_Clubsport

*Everyday racers*

Driving a racing car on the road – Porsche turned this idea into reality in the 1950s with the 550, and in the mid-1960s with the 904. The magic word since the late 1980s has been 'Clubsport'.

The Porsche 911 Carrera Clubsport - or CS - based on the Carrera 3.2, came without rear seats, underfloor coating, air-conditioning, power seats and electrically operated windows in 1987–88. The window cranks and the textile straps for opening the doors became, and remain to this day, much-loved and oft-quoted details of this rough diamond of a Porsche, which was 50 kilos lighter than its standard-production counterpart. The Clubsport ran 20 millimetres closer to the road, featured a locking differential, a shorter axle ratio and lighter wheels. Lighter inlet valves made the 231 hp engine respond more spontaneously to the throttle, and maximum revs increased by 300. This 911 Carrera Clubsport was a rarity, with only 189 coupés and one Targa produced.

Even rarer was the 928 S4 Clubsport, of which a total of 19 were made from April 1988. From 1993, the 968 Clubsport delighted the transaxle community, and the idea of a racing car as a zippy means of commuting to the office lived on until the 991 generation of the 911. As an option, Porsche delivered the Clubsport models with a screw-in roll-over bar, a fire extinguisher, a multi-point safety belt and an emergency electrics master switch. The racing kit, like the sports seats, came at no extra cost. Even sporting this racing outfit, the Clubsport Porsche retained approval for road traffic (at least in Europe).

It was only with the latest generation of the 911 GT2 RS Clubsport and the 718 Cayman GT4 Clubsport that the CS-Porsches became too radical to be let loose on public roads and were only permitted on race circuits. Yet, there is still plenty of opportunity: Some 650 Porsche clubs with more than 600,000 members around the world organise events guaranteed to raise the pulse and adrenalin level of 'Porscheans' with sporting ambitions. Everything is possible, from driver training over slaloms and sprints to endurance races. That's ClubSport.

___ A 1985 pre-production G-Series 911 Carrera 3.2 Clubsport in the museum workshop in Stuttgart-Zuffenhausen. This 911, approved for road use, was also fit for club racing.

Mitarbeiter - Info
PORSCHE
PORSCHE
turbo
911 Turbo

# 73_ Porsche dual-clutch gearbox

*A belated triumph*

The Porsche dual-clutch gearbox (or PDK, short for 'Porsche Doppelkupplungsgetriebe'): three out of four Porsches delivered in 2019 featured it. PDK allows fast, fluid gear changes with an uninterrupted flow of power, better acceleration and lower fuel consumption than manual or conventional automatic gearboxes.

What is a sought-after feature today took off with a bit of a rocky start. For their 1978-79 Type 995 'future sports car' concept, Porsche rediscovered the idea of a gearbox that could be shifted under load, which dated from 1964. This made the racing department prick up their ears. The theory offered the prospect of huge advantages for turbo engines, as the driver would be able to shift gears with the throttle pedal pressed to the floor. Hence, turbo pressure would be retained.

On the racetracks, however, the results were sobering. The PDK weighed 40 kilos more than a conventional racing transmission and its hydraulics consumed 20 hp. The first attempts to synchronise the two clutches mechanically in the days of fledgling electronics resulted in some hair-raising moments. The first race outing at Imola on September 16, 1984, ended with clutch failure after two laps. Hans-Joachim Stuck and Derek Bell scored the only victory in a world championship event at Monza with PDK on April 20, 1986. But the double clutch gearbox remained problematic and the drivers didn't trust it. For the last race of the year contested at Fuji in Japan, Stuck and Bell were expected to compete with still-evolving ABS technology as well as PDK in their Porsche 962C. They tried to persuade the head of development Helmuth Bott to throw both experimental devices out of the car. Bott refused. He gave them a choice: one of the two had to stay. As ABS seemed the riskier of the two, they stuck with PDK – their race ended shortly after the start with broken half-shafts.

___ The beginnings of high-tech: an early Porsche dual-clutch gearbox PDK for the 962 C racing prototype on the testbed in Weissach in 1985.

PDK disappeared from motorsports with the temporary halt of Porsche's works involvement in racing in the late 1980s. However, thanks to rapid progress in electronics and hardware, this ingenious transmission later enjoyed a renaissance. In 2008, the 911 Carrera and Carrera S came with PDK, and it was to be found in some series-production Panameras in 2009. The beginning of a belated triumph.

# 74_ The Home of Rennsport

*Made in Flacht*

A brief explanation of some names: the Porsche development centre is situated about a kilometre west of the town of Weissach, a name that is now famous in the world of motoring. Part of the development centre includes a large testing site with the test track. Only a hundred metres from the southern end of the test track is the northernmost edge of Flacht, a village of 3,000 people (now a district of Weissach). Thus, the hairpin corner near these houses is called the Flachter Spitze ('Flacht Point').

Over the decades, attentive observers have often spotted a little sticker on Porsche racing cars: 'Made in Flacht'. This has historical reasons. Ferry Porsche first broke ground for the building of the Weissach R&D centre on October 16, 1961. A year later, experimental cars were taken through their paces on the skidpad. By the mid-1960s, Porsche had erected the first primitive hangars, just a stone's throw or two north of Flacht. Porsche employees first worked on tanks for the German army here. Then the motorsports crew from Zuffenhausen arrived, preparing their racing cars for test drives, and parking exhausted 910s, 908s and 917s next to the 'tank hall'. In 1971, the test and race department moved from Zuffenhausen to Flacht, took over the hall and set up their offices in an old shack next to it.

The Rennsport headquarters in Flacht and the R&D centre close to Weissach were situated about 800 metres apart. Hence, the motorsports team soon became known as the 'Flachters'. Flacht put in a growth spurt in 2007, with the inauguration of a 12,000-square-metre motorsports base, which further grew into the impressive Flacht racing centre in anticipation of Porsche's return to prototype sports in 2014. Over the years, 'Made in Flacht', once a humorous greeting sent from the motor racing department to colleagues at the Weissach R&D centre in the form of a sticker on racing cars, has become a designation of origin for especially sporty Porsches since 2016.

__ Flacht in 1986. A driver takes a close look at the rear of a 961 for Le Mans. There is a subtle difference: the racing cars come from Flacht, but the massive R&D centre is in Weissach.

Shell
BILSTEIN
BOSCH
SCHMITTHELM
Turbolader
PORSCHE
Shell
MARTINI
BB PW 669

# 75_ Porsche Spyder

*Spyder engine? 911 GT1 98 Spyder?*

The Porsche AG company archive contains a drawing dating from 22 December, 1953. It is the first drawing of a Porsche Spyder, and surprisingly, this 'Type 550 Spyder' has a roof. However, after the first two prototypes, the roof would disappear. The engine retained its position between the cockpit and the rear axle, and from 1954 every mid-engined Porsche without a fixed roof was a 'Porsche Spyder'. So far, so good. But here are two less well-known Spyder stories.

Porsche's engine specialist Valentin Schäffer explained to the author in January 2018 that there was a 'Spyder engine' – a special version of the Carrera engine (Type 547) that the factory planted in its own Spyders in the 1950s and early 1960s. Like all Type 547s, the Spyder engine was air-cooled, featured four overhead camshafts controlled by vertical shafts, two valves per cylinder and double ignition. But Schäffer explained: 'The performance of the Spyder engines was about 20 per cent higher than that of the Carrera engines thanks to higher revs and compression, a modified cam height and valve control, as well as valve spring tension, adjustments to the inlet and outlet ducts, an alteration of the ignition timing, carburettor and exhaust system.'

The racing engineer Norbert Singer, who was involved in a number of victories between 1970 and 2004 and is regarded as a leading aerodynamics expert, had the following to add: 'Spyders are, in principle, superior to their roofed cousins in terms of downforce, which is so important for road stability and cornering speed. The reason is that the airflow passes over a coupé roof at higher speed and thus creates uplift.' While working on his last Le Mans winner, the 911 GT1 98 Coupé, the roof of a wind-tunnel model had to be removed during a repair. Singer was curious and placed this improvised 'Spyder' in the wind tunnel only to discover that the downforce was ten per cent higher than before.

___ This drawing, dated December 22, 1953, is the first with the subtitle 'Spyder'. The roof quickly disappeared, but the mid-engine principle has remained to this day.

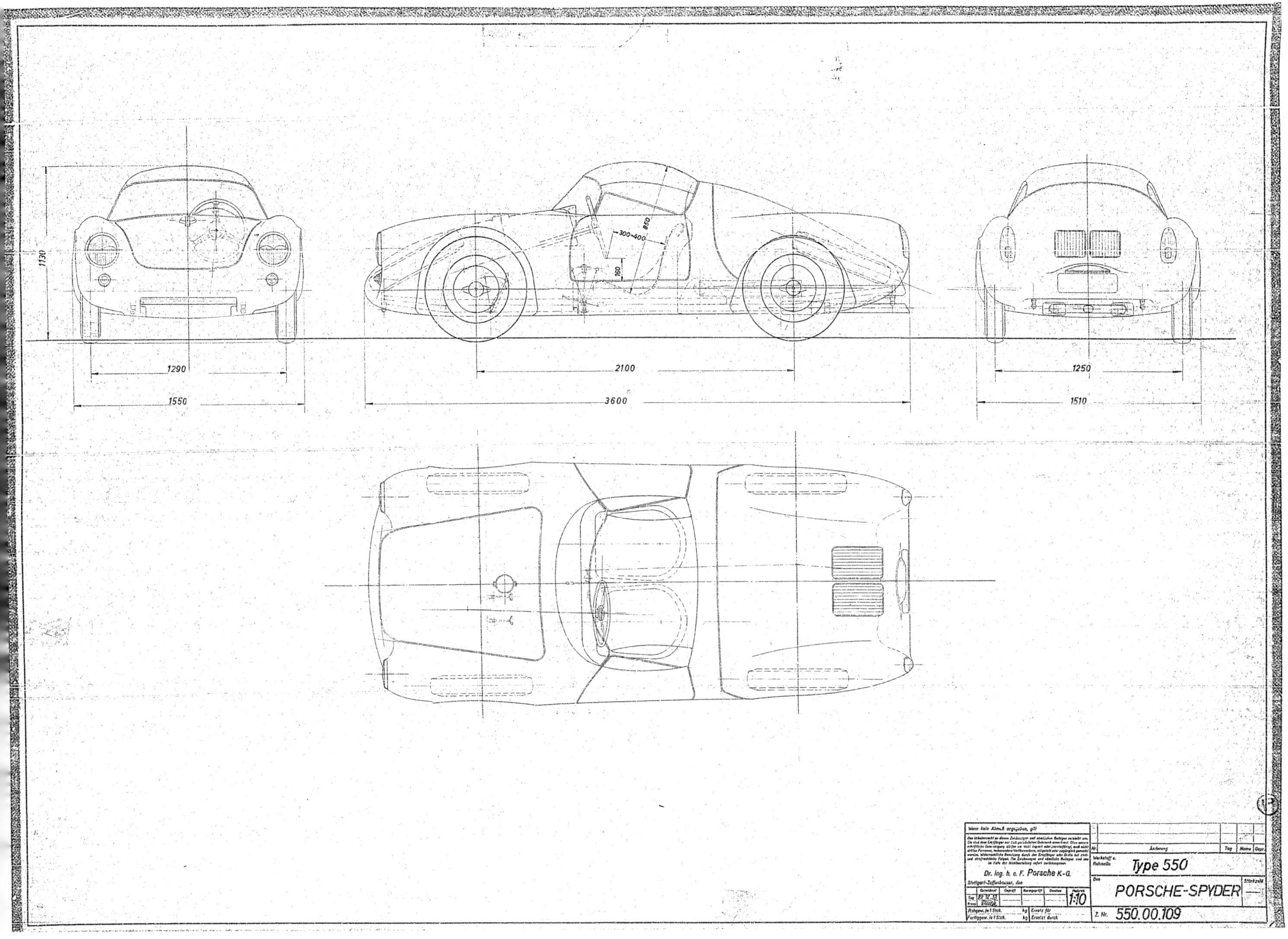
1130
850
300-400
160
1290
1550
2100
3600
1250
1510
Wenn kein Abmaß angegeben, gilt
Dr. Ing. h. c. F. Porsche K-G.
Stuttgart-Zuffenhausen, den
Gezeichnet
Geprüft
Normgeprüft
Gesehen
Maßstab
1:10
Tag
22.12.53
Rohgew. je 1 Stck. kg
Fertiggew. je 1 Stck. kg
Ersatz für
Ersetzt durch
Nr.
Änderung
Tag
Name
Gepr.
Werkstoff u. Rohmaße
Type 550
Ben
PORSCHE-SPYDER
Stückzahl
Z. Nr.
550.00.109

The open 718 RS 61 Spyder was run at Le Mans in 1961 and won the 2-litre class ahead of the No. 32 Porsche 718 RS 61 Coupé.

30
32
33
S-LX600

# 76__RS & RSR

*RennSportRennwagen*

RS stands for RennSport: a.k.a. motor racing. Ferry Porsche is said to have personally given the distinction of these two letters to the highly successful Porsche 550 A Spyder of 1954. The next RSs were the 718 RS-K and 718 RS 60/61. The mid-engine racing car, which Porsche fielded in the USA from late 2005 until 2008, was dubbed the RS Spyder. In Class 2 of the Le Mans prototypes, this 500 hp Porsche proved almost unbeatable, upholding the long tradition of the 935s and 962s.

An RS line has also graced the 911 model family since 1973, beginning with the Porsche 911 Carrera RS 2.7. RS stands for low weight, plenty of horsepower, highly sophisticated chassis, suspension and transmission, and exceptional aerodynamics: the duck tail on the engine cover of the RS 2.7 now has cult status. The RS derivates of the Nine-Elevens all came with ideal prerequisites to be converted into racing cars. And this transformation turned an RS into an RSR, which means RennsportRennwagen and a lot of radical technical modifications.

A cleverly conceived RS paved the way for a race winning RSR. In this way, the RS 2.7, powered with 210 hp and weighing about 1,110 kilos, was converted within two years into the 911 Carrera RSR 2.1 Turbo with 500 hp for a mere 750 kilograms. At the same time, the production numbers shrank considerably: 1,525 units of the RS 2.7 were made, whereas the RSR 2.1 Turbo reached a grand total of four.

Porsche recently showed just how far this transformation can be taken with the 991-Type 911 RSR for endurance racing. The aim was to put a large diffuser under the tail for increased downforce and reduced tyre wear. So without further ado, the engine moved to its new position in front of the rear axle for the 2017 campaign.

__ The 2020 Porsche 911 RSR features a mid-ship engine. This leaves room for the massive rear diffuser and improves the weight balance.

PORSCHE
PORSCHE
RSR
CHOPARD
Mobil 1
MICHELIN

# 77_The Schüttgut

*Home*

Porsche is Stuttgart-Zuffenhausen, the site of the main factory. Porsche is also the family name. This name is closely associated with two places: The villa in Feuerbacher Strasse in Stuttgart built in 1923 by the patriarch Ferdinand Porsche (1875–1951), and the Schüttgut, a grand, centuries-old farmhouse and estate near Zell am See in Austria's Pinzgau region.

Ferdinand Porsche bought the estate high on a slope in the Schüttdorf district in 1941 as a place of retreat and a base in his beloved Austria. His son Ferry (1909–1998) had discovered this gem while on a test drive with an early Beetle prototype. Ferdinand's daughter, Louise Piëch (1904–1999), and Ferry took their families to the safety of this estate in 1943. Thus, the third generation including Ferdinand Alexander "F. A." Porsche (1935–2012), Wolfgang Porsche (*1943) and Ferdinand Piëch (1937–2019) spent years of their childhood at the Schüttgut, which became the family homestead.

It remained the family's residence after the company's return to Stuttgart in 1949 – which may not come as a total surprise. After all, the mountain roads offered outstanding testing grounds for sports cars. Ferdinand used the Katschberg Pass, 90 minutes to the south, as one of his favoured test routes. At the tender age of 18, Ferdinand Piëch wrote off his first 356 on the Lueg Pass – according to legend he was attempting to beat the record time for the journey from Salzburg to Dellach set by his mother! Wolfgang Porsche calls the Glockner Pass his home turf.

The family's involvement in the region goes back decades. The Porsches bought the airfield at Zell am See and a business park, which is now the home of Porsche Design, only a few hundred metres from the Schüttgut. They operate a ferry service on Lake Zell, mountain cable cars and a luxury hotel, and are involved in farming and forestry. Fundamental decisions were taken at the Schüttgut. It was here, in 1972, that the Porsche and Piëch families decided to withdraw from managing the company. Wolfgang Porsche acquired the estate, which he regards as his home, in 2003.

___ Ferdinand Porsche bought the Schüttgut in 1941. This grand house above Zell am See in Austria became a home for generations of the family.

# 78_ Fuchs Rim

*Aluminium cult*

The wheel of a sportscar: an unsprung rotating mass. The smaller the mass, the more spontaneous the springs and shock absorbers react, and the less it hinders acceleration, braking and cornering in – let's say – an early 911. This is why, at the very start of the 911 adventure, Porsche searched for a light but enormously stable alternative to a wheel of steel.

The solution rumbled across various testing grounds for tanks: Porsche was developing an armoured vehicle suitable for transport by air for the German army. Otto Fuchs KG in Meinerzhagen 70 km east of Cologne – a specialist in high-end alloys – produced the aluminium road wheel for the combat vehicle. Porsche approached Fuchs, who accepted the challenge and presented a firework of innovation, inventing a new and very complex production process. Over 58 stages, an aluminium blank sheet was turned into a single-piece lightweight alloy wheel. The Fuchs rim was the first forged light-metal alloy wheel to be produced in large numbers for road use.

After initial work by the Porsche designer Heinrich Klie and Fuchs KG, it was none other than F. A. Porsche who finalised the styling of the five-spoke wheel. The 'clover-leaf design' 4.5 x 15 Fuchs wheel for 165 VR15 tyres first adorned the especially sporty 911 S in 1966. It saved about three kilograms per wheel compared to its steel counterpart. Porsche also used the light 'windmill' wheel later on for the 914 mid-engine sports car and the transaxle 944.

The launch of the third generation of 911s in 1989 seemed to signal the end of the cult Fuchs rim on the 911. However, ongoing demand from Porsche drivers finally bore fruit when Otto Fuchs KG began producing forged design classics again in 2009. Now, the Fuchs rim is once again available in contemporary designs and the required huge dimensions for several Porsche models.

___ The 'windmill' wheel: a classic forged design, lighter and more stable than steel, corrosion-proof and perfectly balanced. A must on many models, including the Porsche 911 Carrera RS 2.7.

Carrera

# 79_ Vintage Porsches

*Treasures on wheels*

Some Porsches are born to be rare, conceived with painstaking dedication, and made in small series. Placed like an exclamation mark at the end of a series, like the 911 Turbo 3.6 'slant nose'. Just 76 were made in 1994. Reminiscent of great names, like the 911 Speedster from 2019, limited to an edition of 1,948 cars. Let loose on the roads as super sports cars with extreme technology, like the 2003 Carrera GT. Or made as homologation specials like 911 GT1 Strasse. Porsche made 21 road legal examples of their Le Mans contender in 1997.

Porsches such as these are pursued and coveted by fans and investors. As you would expect, treasures on wheels come at eye-watering prices. Porsche offered the GT1 Strasse from 1997 at around 1.5 million Deutschmarks. In 2017, one of these racers fetched 5.7 million USD at auction. In 2016, Jerry Seinfeld had his 1955 550 Spyder auctioned for 5.3 million USD. For the 956 that won Le Mans in 1982, the auctioneer's gavel rapped down in 2015 at a little over ten million U.S. dollars. The Swiss racing driver Jo Siffert's short-tail 917, which Steve McQueen borrowed in 1970 for the filming of his 'Le Mans' movie, fetched more than 14 million USD in 2017. And in 2012, the 917/10 that proved unbeatable in America in 1972 changed hands for more than four million dollars.

The figures are not always as dizzying as this, but where vintage racing cars are concerned, nothing is to be had for less than a few hundred thousand dollars. Provided, that is, they are a sought-after model, they are genuine and were demonstrably driven at famous races by famous pilots. Their technical condition is also of interest but does not seem to a critical factor – although the advice of an experienced collector is: 'Never buy a cheap historic Porsche. In the end, restoring it will cost twice as much as what you would have paid for one in good condition.'

___ Porsche built a series of 21 911 GT1s for the road. Sold from the factory in 1997 for about 1.5 million Deutschmarks, a GT1 fetched 5.7 million USD at auction in 2017.

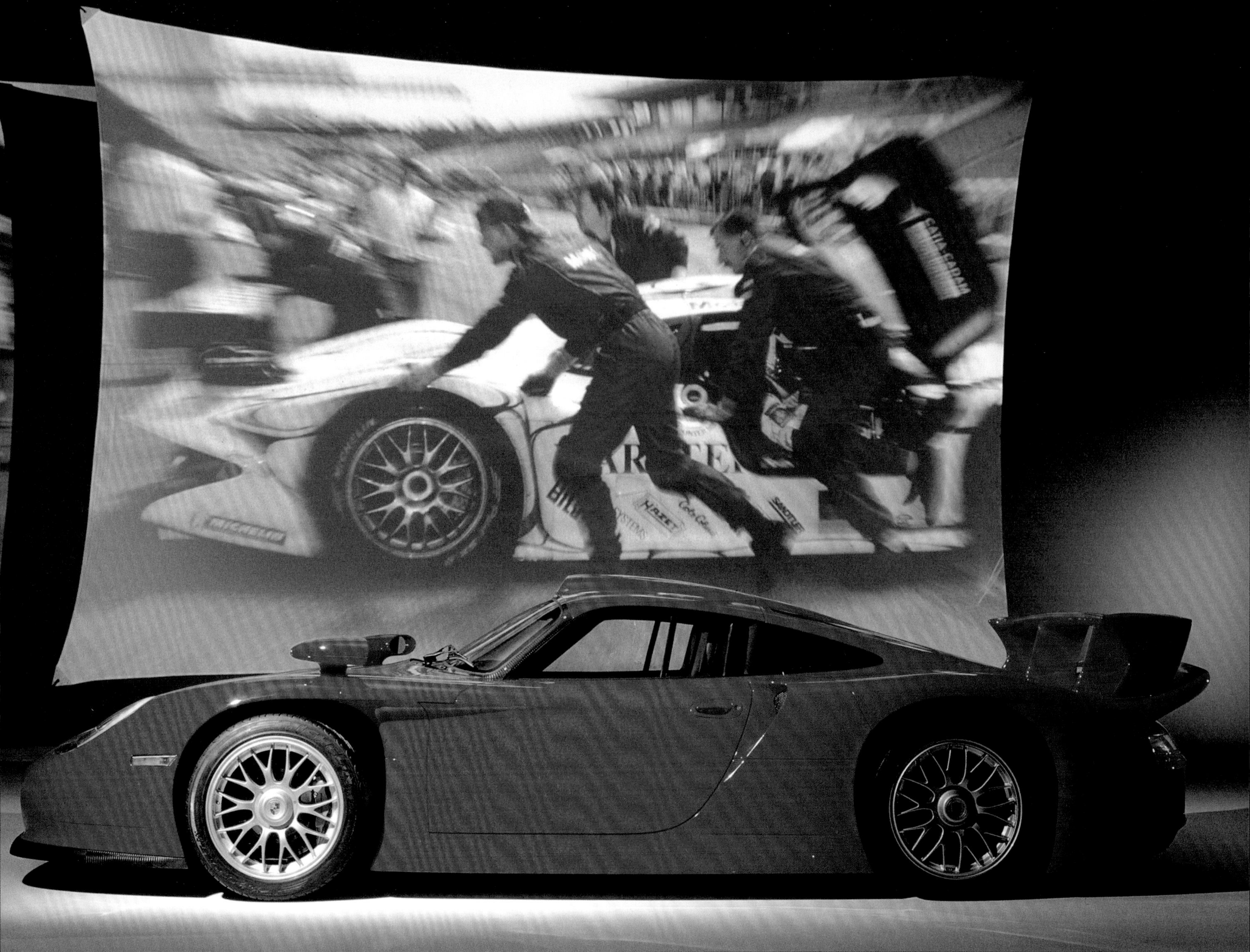
MICHELIN
HAZET

Weissach skidpad, 1976, foreman Hubert Mimler at the wheel of the 936. With him (right to left) are race director Peter Falk, engine chief Peter Hensler, and head of R&D Helmuth Bott. On the far left: Helmut Flegl, head of the 936 project.

# PIT LANE & EXECUTIVE FLOOR

STAHLWILLE

# 80_ Bernhard Blank and Rupprecht von Senger

*Swiss courage*

Ferry Porsche, two bold Swiss men and a daring Swiss lady. This was the start of the Porsche 356's global success story. First, Ferry Porsche conceived the sports car he dreamed of and built it himself. This was in summer 1948 – at a time when the idea of producing an expensive sports car called for a great deal of visionary courage.

A Swiss, Rupprecht von Senger, bought Porsche's 356 No. 1 prototype on the very day it gained road approval. He obviously believed in the sports car and made it available to Swiss journalists for test drives on the occasion of the Swiss Grand Prix. What's more, von Senger brokered an order for more sports cars from the factory in Gmünd, sweetened by an advance payment of 100,000 Swiss francs as a little boost for the start-up. The money came from the hotelier and businessman Bernhard Blank, another man of vision. Blank promptly turned a part of the foyer of his Hotel Europe in Zurich into a Porsche showroom. Together with Ferry's sister Louise Piëch, he then reserved booth number eleven at the automobile salon in Geneva, where they displayed a 356/2 cabriolet and a coupé made in Gmünd from March 17, 1949.

It was also Bernhard Blank who supplied the first series-built 356/2 to a customer in spring 1949. He sold the cabriolet to Jolanda von Tschudi, whose name also appears in reports as Jolantha or Yolande Tschudi. Frau von Tschudi was free of material worries, and devoted much of her time, among other activities, to extreme gliding. She undertook and survived many a daring exploit. In the late 1940s, she engaged in expeditions by plane (with an engine in this case) in North and West Africa, and her name is associated with a book about North African cave painting. While Frau von Tschudi enjoyed her cabriolet, Bernhard Blank operated as the sales partner for Porsche until spring 1951, when AMAG took over this business in Switzerland for decades to come.

___ Bernhard Blank at the wheel of a 356/2 Beutler Cabriolet at the Geneva Salon in 1949, with Louise Piëch in the passenger seat. This was the first appearance of a Porsche at a trade fair.

# 81_Fritz Enzinger

*Friendly face of success*

Fritz Enzinger is the vice president of Porsche motorsports and coordinates the Volkswagen Group's worldwide racing activities. The native of Austria makes major decisions every day, and he performs his powerful job in his very own way: with friendly composure – and extraordinary determination. At Le Mans in 2017, one of the two factory-run Porsche 919 Hybrids mounted a risky charge back up the order over 20-and-a-half hours following a repair, ploughing through the field from 56th place to first. Why did Enzinger decide to take the risk instead of opting for a safe result? 'We had to,' he says. This man has a competitive spirit in his DNA.

Born in 1956 and trained as a mechanical engineer, he came to Porsche in November 2011 after 30 years with BMW. The aim was to reinstate Porsche at the top of motorsport, and he started 'with a blank sheet of paper on a greenfield site,' he recalls. No buildings, no personnel, no experience with the technology of Le Mans class-one prototypes. Enzinger established a new team, recruiting seven out of ten of its members externally. Outsourcing was out of the question, because only a factory squad has the full support of the entire company, and the right spirit only exists in a team that has grown together. Ultimately, 200 people worked on the new racing car. Right from the start, the motto was to build a lightning-fast contender rather than play safe. The 919 Hybrid represented a radical design approach. All of this happened under time pressure. The roll-out was in June 2013, with the usual teething problems around the car: 'Le Mans 2014 was too early for us.' But the daring approach proved successful. Porsche won Le Mans in 2015, 2016 and 2017, and claimed the manufacturer's and driver's world championship titles three years straight.

After this brilliant success, Enzinger turned his attention to the next challenge. With Porsche now focusing on Formula E, his task was to merge the team of the LMP programme with the GT motorsports team, which had been independent up until then. He succeeded. In 2019, Porsche won every major title in the GT pro-class with the 911 RSR and put the 99X Electric on the track. Enzinger managed this with quiet determination. And a smile.

___ As vice president of motor racing, Fritz Enzinger won at Le Mans three times with the factory team and netted six World Endurance Championship titles. Since 2019, he has been at the helm of motorsports for the Volkswagen group.

PORSCHE
MOTORSPORT
PORSCHE
MOTORSPORT
BOSS
HUGO BOSS

# 82__ Richard von Frankenberg

*Schreckenstein, the all-rounder*

The early morning banks of fog may be soupy, but that is no reason at all to approach the fast bends of Le Mans with hesitancy. Indeed, the driver sees nothing yet keeps the pedal to the metal. Suddenly, a patch of grass looms into sight on the right. Now, and not one fraction of a second sooner, the foot hits the brake pedal. This is how Richard von Frankenberg described one of the reasons why he and Paul Frère won their class in 1953 driving a tiny hardtop 550 prototype.

'Schreckenstein' (which literally means 'rock of fright') was the nickname rivals gave the aristocrat. Born in 1922 and baptised Richard-Alexander Ruthard Edi Wolf Eberhard von Frankenberg und Ludwigsdorff, he grew to know no fear of speed in the heat of the competition. In 1951, on the oval circuit of Monthléry near Paris, he and four colleagues set several world records, including 10,968 kilometres in 72 hours in a 1.5-litre 356. After his initial class victory at Le Mans, he scored two further class wins at the French classic and at the Mille Miglia in Italy. Schreckenstein was crowned German racing champion in 1955, survived a spectacular accident with Mickey Mouse in 1956 (our story 4) and set more speed records with two teammates at Monza driving a 356 A Carrera Speedster a year later.

Off the racetracks, Frankenberg was one of the great all-rounders who helped shape the Porsche company in the early years. He pursued his passion for journalism from an early age, working for the German-language service of the BBC during World War II. He founded the Porsche customer magazine Christophorus in 1952 with the graphic artist Erich Strenger, wrote for major specialist journals and enjoyed popularity as a television and radio presenter. As a driver-cum-author, Frankenberg wrote dozens of books under the pseudonyms Herbert A. Quint and Alexander Borelius, some of them as a co-author. Richard von Frankenberg hung up his helmet as a works driver in 1960 but occupied the editor-in-chief's chair at Christophorus until his death in an accident on the Autobahn in November 1973.

__ Not in a racing car, for once: Richard von Frankenberg in 1966 during a trip with his wife Helga. Their daughter Stephanie sits in the back seat.

# 83__Maximilian Edwin Hoffman

*Nothing by halves*

Maximilian Edwin Hoffman deserves a biography of at least 400 pages. Here is the short version in less than 300 words. Born in Vienna in 1904 to a Catholic mother and a Jewish father, Maximilian Hoffmann fled from the Nazis in 1938, made it first to the Netherlands, then South Africa and finally to New York City. He settled there in 1941, and in 1947 established Hoffman Motors (he had shed one 'n' on the journey) and was soon a successful dealer in luxury European automobiles.

With incredible energy, Hoffman built up a sales network on the East Coast. Its heart beat in a showroom at the corner of Park Avenue and 56th Street, designed by the star architect Frank Lloyd Wright, who was also crazy about cars. In October 1950, Hoffman met Ferdinand Porsche at the Paris motor show. They hit it off, and three 356s crossed the Atlantic that same month. Hoffman had his finger on the pulse of what his clientele wanted. He suggested, with some insistence, that Zuffenhausen produce the America Roadster (1952) and the 356 Speedster of 1954 because a) his customers were mad about racing cars, and b) he was well aware of the proven saying: 'Win on Sunday, sell on Monday'. It was also Hoffman's demand for a Porsche crest that added fuel to Dr Domnick's idea (our story 61).

Under Hoffman, for whom John von Neumann handled business on the US West Coast, Porsche sales went through the roof: in 1952, one in five 356s went to the USA; by 1955 it was one in two. As a businessman, Mr Hoffman, as he was generally known, was extremely hard-nosed. Even by failing to purchase just a single screw from him for your Porsche meant losing the warranty. Ferdinand Porsche's private secretary Ghislaine Kaes described Hoffman as an extremely confident negotiator when it came to his share of the sales revenue. But for Kaes, he was also '[...] a great man in his kingdom [...]. Hoffman handed over his kingdom to the Porsche of America Corporation in return for a golden handshake in autumn 1964. He died in 1981 in the USA.

__ Maximilian E. Hoffman in a Glöckler Porsche in 1951. Hoffman was inducted into the Automotive Hall of Fame in 2003, with the citation that he single-handedly established car imports to the USA.

81
84
BATH HOUSE
DUNLOP

# 84_ Roland Kussmaul

*Master of all trades*

This book is about stories, not CVs, but we will say this much: Roland Kussmaul was born in 1942, graduated from university as a mechanical engineer and worked for Porsche from 1969 to 2009. In his Porsche days, Kussmaul was a test engineer, racing and rally driver, a test driver, co-driver and on occasion the technical manager at large-scale operations such as Porsche's Paris–Dakar Rally campaigns. In addition to motorsports, Kussmaul played a leading role in developing such icons as the 964 generation 911 RS, the first 911 GT3 and the Carrera GT of 2003. Today, he lives with his wife and dog in the quiet town of Eberdingen near Stuttgart.

Many items in his home are souvenirs from Africa and his Safari Rally days of the 1970s. A vintage 911 RS and a rather wild 914/6 relax in the garage. Kussmaul has tales to tell: of a stationary and rather hair-raising 30-hour test with the 956, of driving with Waldegård in East Africa, of the 20,000-kilometre rally around Australia in a 924, of developing the 959 for the Dakar Rally and the 961 for Le Mans. So which one shall we choose from these hundreds of stories? Perhaps Le Mans in 1983, when the 956 under his care rolled over the finishing line with a dying engine and won (our story 19)?

Let's take Paris–Dakar in 1986. On January 20, a few hundred kilometres from the finish, a one-two result looked likely for René Metge and Jacky Ickx with their 959s after more than 14,000 bone-crunching kilometres through Africa. Kussmaul and his co-driver Hendrik Unger trailed them in a 959, crammed to the roof with spare parts. Metge and Ickx sank their beautiful 959s to the axles in the mud of the Senegal Delta. Kussmaul was soon on the spot, after all, he was running in a sensational fourth place overall with his 'chase car'. While trying to tow Metge's car out of the mud, his Porsche got stuck in the sludge. Kussmaul dived in, dug as if his life depended on it and got both Ickx and Metge going again. He stayed behind, exhausted and covered in filth. In the night, Roland was overcome by a raging fever and hallucinations. Rough-and-ready medical treatment got him back on his feet. Metge won the rally ahead of Ickx. Kussmaul finished sixth in his 959 'chase car'.

— Roland Kussmaul loading his 911 SC 4x4 at the Paris–Dakar Rally in 1984. He developed this rally car and was responsible for the technology of the desert Porsches.

TEXACO
Rothmans
Rothmans
PORSCHE

# 85__Hubert Mimler

*Fastest of all taxi drivers*

The story of the world's fastest taxi driver began on April 1, 1951. This was the day that the young mechanic Hubert Mimler first stepped through the gates of the factory in Zuffenhausen, where Porsche had been assembling the 356 for a year. Mimler quickly worked his way up in the test and development department, and after the move to Weissach, he was promoted as foreman with responsibility for about 100 staff.

From day one, he devoted his love and passion to the racing cars, and from 1954 onwards he had the privilege to drive the 550s, 718s, 904s and all that he helped to create. More often than not, he was the first man in the cockpit of the new competition Porsches. Mimler took the wheel of everything and even steered the fearsome 917/10 around the Weissach track in July 1971. That same year, the short-tail 917 in which Pedro Rodríguez and Jackie Oliver had won the legendary 1,000-kilometre race at Spa, was returned to Porsche. Mimler put a second seat into the 600 hp beast. And this was the birth of the Porsche racing taxi. From then on, celebrities from the realms of sports, politics and show business queued up at the door of the 800-kilo rocket, eager to be taken around the Weissach circuit by Mimler. He didn't hold back. The 917 reached 300 kph even on the short straights. Most passengers lost colour in their cheeks after two laps of the 2.75-kilometre circuit and threw in the towel shortly afterwards.

When this 917 rolled into the museum in 1977, Mimler took over a 935 with 650 hp. Racing driver Jochen Mass had once characterised the handling of the world-championship-winning brute as follows: 'In this car, you get full-body aquaplaning even on the straight.' Mimler always kept the 935 under control; there are no records of accidents of the world's fastest taxi driver. On days with a lively attendance of VIP guests, he spent many strenuous hours in the cockpit. When a motorsports journal asked him how he maintained his exceptional stamina, he showed his true Swabian colours. He kept fit, he said, by building houses with his sons-in-law. Hubert Mimler died in summer 1982.

___ Hubert Mimler during a test session with an early 904 Carrera GTS in winter 1963–64. Mimler had a reputation as an excellent technician, foreman – and as the world's fastest taxi driver...

# 86__ Karl Rabe

*Beetle, Gmünd and 356*

Karl Rabe displayed such great talent that managing director Ferdinand Porsche appointed the 24-year-old as 'chief designer for cars' at the Austro Daimler Motoren AG in Wiener Neustadt in 1919. After Porsche and young Rabe created vehicles such as the racing car 'Sascha', their ways parted. They would meet again years later when Rabe joined Porsche's design and construction office as head of design in Stuttgart in 1931.

They were a brilliant duo. Rabe captured Porsche's creativity in drawings, oversaw the work at the drawing boards and became Ferdinand Porsche's close confidant. In 1934, Porsche was commissioned by the Automobile Industry Association of the German Reich to design and make a people's car, a 'Volkswagen'. Rabe led the design of the rotund vehicle, which went on to make history after 1945 as the 'Beetle'. The following years were marked by the development of war machinery and the relocation of most of Porsche's staff to quite basic premises in Gmünd, Austria. After the end of the war, the French imprisoned Ferdinand Porsche from August 1945 until July 1947, while his son Ferry was interned until August, 1946. The work at Gmünd continued under Ferry's sister Louise Piëch and Rabe. In his curriculum vitae, he recorded about the second half of 1945: '[...] technical management of the operation in Gmünd [was] entirely in my hands, and my most important intention was to retain and expand this group [...] with its valuable employees.'

In 1947, with Rabe heading the engineering team, the project gained momentum that would turn Porsche from an engineering office into a sports car manufacturer. Rabe recalled the '[...] development of our own sports car, Type 356, first of all as an open model. Manufacture of this vehicle individually, including the bodywork, with the very limited means of production at hand in Gmünd. This car was the precursor of the sports car that was later made in Stuttgart.' Rabe became a member of the management board in 1951 and remained Ferry Porsche's personal adviser until he retired in 1965. 'Father Rabe', as he was known at Porsche thanks to his concern for the welfare of his employees, died in 1968.

__ The Austrian Karl Rabe in the 1960s. He worked with Ferdinand Porsche from 1919 as head designer and remained one of the leading technical brains at the company until 1965.

# 87_Franz Xaver Reimspiess

*Beetle engine and Porsche crest*

Franz Xaver Reimspiess, born in 1900 in Austria's Wiener Neustadt, joined Ferdinand Porsche's design office in Stuttgart in September 1934. Porsche and his chief engineer Karl Rabe knew Reimspiess from their early years at Austro Daimler, where he had delivered mail as a 15-year-old and soon amazed the engineers with his technical drawings.

Reimspiess went to university and became one of Porsche's leading designers. Ferdinand Porsche's son Ferry recalled in the company magazine Christophorus in 1981: 'One of his special characteristics was as follows: if he was drawing, for example, the Auto Union racing engine, first he drew a draft, then fixed a sheet over it and did a second draft. Then he'd place a sheet over it again – and on every sheet the engine became smaller and more compact. This showed patience and a striving for perfection that I rarely ever encountered later.'

Reimspiess had many talents. In 1936, he designed the Volkswagen logo of 'V and W in a circle', which Porsche registered as a trademark in 1938. The logo is used to this day and was last modernised in September 2019. Also in 1936, Reimspiess designed the flat-four engine for the 'people's car' that was eventually manufactured as the 'Beetle' 21.5 million times. He was awarded a bonus of 100 Reichsmarks for this epoch-making design. During the war, Reimspiess was involved in Porsche's unsuccessful attempts to design tanks for the Nazis. After the restart in Stuttgart in 1950, he played a leading role in the making of sports cars as chief engineer, and in 1952 he designed in passing, with Ferry Porsche, another globally renowned trademark: the Porsche crest. In a laudatory speech for Reimspiess in 1968, Richard von Frankenberg revealed another talent: 'What else can he do? He can double-tone whistle. When he's in a good mood, Reimspiess is one of those people with a wicked sense of humour.' Franz Xaver Reimspiess retired in 1966. He died in 1979.

___ Franz Xaver Reimspiess in a photo dating from 1965: a brilliant designer who invented the Volkswagen logo, the Beetle engine and contributed to the design of the Porsche crest.

# 88_ Valentin Schäffer

*'I'm thinking of 1,000 hp'*

American motor journals loved to call Valentin Schäffer the 'turbo wizard'. Schäffer is the man who made Porsche's turbocharged engines run and win in the early 1970s. He worked on the most powerful racing engines on the test bench, in the workshops, in dialogue with the designers and at the racetracks.

Sent on an investigative tour in the pre-turbo days by Ferdinand Piëch, who was always looking for higher performance and lower lap times, Schäffer visited the turbo specialists at the Eberspächer factory. Asked what kind of power he envisaged for a Porsche turbo motor, he innocently replied: 'I'm thinking of 1,000 hp.' When Schäffer then explained in confidence that the race department needed a bit of grunt for their Type 917 racing car, the Eberspächer people overcame their shock and were extremely enthusiastic. As is well-known, the twelve-cylinder, twin-turbo engine of the unbeatable 917/30 in 1973 generated about 1,100 horsepower: A highlight for Schäffer, who headed the development and maintenance of the racing engines in the test department since 1966.

Valentin Schäffer had joined Porsche as a 24-year-old engine mechanic in 1955, and was soon involved in developing the 'Fuhrmann engine'. From the later pre-turbo age, some of Schäffer's fondest memories go back to the evolution of the twelve-cylinder, naturally aspirated engine for the 917 in the late 1960s. To be more precise: to the drama of making the central drive gear on the crankshaft survive. Ultimately it would last – though only after a few engines had given up the ghost in a spectacular manner on the test bench. However, the turbo, as he admits, is where his heart lies. 1976 saw the first win for a turbo engine (for Porsche and anyone at all) at Le Mans. In 1980, Hans Mezger as designer and Schäffer in the testing department developed a 2.65-litre turbo with just under 900 hp for Indianapolis. When Porsche pulled out of Indy, this motor found a place behind the cockpit of the 936, then the 956 and the 962, which won record numbers of races and titles. After what would have been a good 1,000 races, Valentin Schäffer headed into retirement in 1991.

__ Two key figures of Porsche racing in conversation in 1987: the 'turbo wizard' Valentin Schäffer (left) and the 'magician of aerodynamics' Norbert Singer.

LOWENBRAU
RACING

# 89_ Peter Werner Schutz

*Lengthened the lifeline*

It is January 1981, and the 50-year-old American Peter Werner Schutz has been Porsche's CEO for three weeks. He's in a meeting with Helmuth Bott, director of development. A wall planner in Bott's office shows the model ranges and their scheduled lifespans: The lifelines of the 924, the forthcoming 944, the 928 and the 911. The 911 line ends in 1984.

Schutz later related how he got up from his chair and extended the 911 line with a marker pen across the wallpaper to the door. And how Bott reacted with relief. Schutz's predecessor Ernst Fuhrmann had announced the end of the 911 and declared the transaxle Porsches to be the future, which had made neither shareholders nor customers happy. Sales figures had plummeted, and the second 'energy crisis' in 1979–80 had accelerated the downward trend. Fuhrmann had to go. His successor Schutz kept the 911 projects going and pushed Porsche's racing activities. The 911 Cabriolet was launched in 1982, and in 1983, the 959 concept car appeared as 'Studie Gruppe B' at the IAA motor show in Frankfurt. Porsche Type 956/962C racers and the TAG Formula 1 engine dominated top-level motorsports. Business in the USA picked up momentum again and became a gold mine at an exchange rate of over three Deutschmarks to the dollar. By 1985–86, Schutz had doubled sales to about 53,000 sports cars. More than half of the Porsches made crossed the Atlantic. While Porsche had earned 10 million Deutschmarks in 1980–81, the figure in 1984–85 was 120 million.

Not much went wrong under Schutz. The PFM 3200 aero-engine was a superb piece of engineering but was launched at the wrong time. The attempt to set up Porsche's own outlets in the USA against the local dealers failed at first. But when the US economy slid into recession in the mid-1980s, Porsche's dependence on the American market proved disastrous for the business. Workers in Zuffenhausen were on short time, and the value of Porsche shares was slashed in half. At the end of 1987, finance manager Heinz Branitzki took over as Porsche's new CEO. Peter W. Schutz returned to the USA to work as a management consultant and lived with his family in Florida, where he died in October 2017 at the age of 87.

__ Peter Werner Schutz in 1985 with his wife Sheila at the race in Le Mans. Schutz gave strong new impetus to Porsche's model policy and to motor racing.

# 90_Alwin Springer

*"Just wanted to see a bit of the world"*

Alwin Springer is a self-made man: Obsessed with technology and pivotal in preparing Porsche race engines to win races and titles in the USA from the 1970s through to the start of the 21st century. A diplomat for whom superficial harmony means nothing, and integrity everything. An entrepreneur who founded Andial in California's Santa Ana in 1975 together with his friends, Arnold Wagner and Dieter Inzenhofer.

Andial quickly grew into the largest independent Porsche representative in North America. Springer looked after the technical side of the business, and racing engines prepared in Santa Ana powered the Porsche 911 RSR, the 935, the 962 and later the 911-GTs to countless triumphs. Springer gained the confidence of racing customers across the USA, to whom he passed on every development following a test phase in the Porsche of Al Holbert, head of sports in the USA. Suppliers pulled out all stops for Andial and Springer. His relations with the highly patriotic and consequently not very Porsche-friendly motorsports authorities in the USA were and are marked by mutual respect.

After the tragic death of Al Holbert in an accident at the end of 1989, and at the wish of management in Weissach, Springer took over the management of Porsche motorsport in America. Although an independent adviser, he succeeded in gaining the trust of Porsche Cars North America, who had been a bit reluctant to deal with the German initially. In 1997, Springer sold his shares in Andial to his two partners and signed a contract with Porsche that made him the boss of Porsche Motorsport North America. He fulfilled this role with dedication, success and great diplomatic skill until his retirement from the front line in February 2004.

To this day, Springer is a consultant to Porsche Motorsport North America, and in all modesty knows his own worth: 'It's not because of my beautiful blue eyes that the Swabians have worked with me for all these years!' An astonishing career that began humbly, when a 22-year-old auto electrician and mechanic from Essen moved to Canada in 1965. Just because he wanted to see a bit of the world.

__ Alwin Springer (right) in 2006 with the racing engineer Norbert Singer. Springer just wanted to see a bit of the world. He ended up as head of Porsche Motorsport in the USA.

PORSCHE
RENNSPORT
REUNION II
Motorsport
RACING
PORSCHE
Motorsport

First victories, last drives, new ideas around the world and through history. Here, a 917/30 with more than 1,200 hp waits for its farewell lap on the Trioval of Talladega, USA.

# HELLO & GOODBYE

ANNISTON
DieHard
CAM2
PORSCHE
6
FIRST NATIONAL CITY
TRAVELERS CHECKS
GOODYEAR

# 91__Rally to the Midnight Sun, 1950

*First factory mission*

June 15 to 18, 1950: the annals of the Porsche Museum record the start of the inaugural Rally to the Midnight Sun as Porsche's first works-supported mission at a motorsport event of international importance. Two brand-new Porsche 356s from Stuttgart, where production had started just three months previously, entered the rally. Prince Joachim zu Fürstenberg and Count Constantin von Berckheim drove a coupé with 1,086 cc, 40 hp and the starting number 58. Günther Count zu Hardenberg and Prince Friedrich zu Fürstenberg shared the cockpit of the cabriolet with the starting number 62. It is almost impossible to piece together what the involvement of the Porsche factory actually was. Did Porsche pay the bill for the frightfully expensive drinks? Or for the tyres and fuel?

Either way, Ferry Porsche was delighted – a contest over 2,250 kilometres with two special stages (39 and 90 kilometres) and a final test of acceleration and braking was exactly to the liking of the company's junior boss. Ferry insisted that a Porsche was not only fast but durable. The required minimum average speed over the distance was 50 kph, and 75 kph for the special stages. Those who were slower received penalty points. It was a devil of a race on gravel tracks, and the press reported averages of over 100 kph. There were a few minor incidents: rolling cars, smashed barn walls, technical breakdowns, and a bus coming opposite the competitors on the 39-kilometre special stage.

In the end, Prince Joachim and Count Constantin won class IV for cars with less than 1.1-litre displacement. But the greatest media attention went to Countess Cecilia Koskull from Stockholm and her co-driver Christina Peyron. Their white 356/2 Coupé from the Gmünd production was considered the most elegant car in the rally. The countess was not averse to putting her foot down: she won the ladies' title and achieved a highly respectable fourth place in the 1.5-litre class. Grus-Olle Persson claimed the first of four overall wins in succession for Porsche in a 356 in 1952.

___ Porsche's first 'factory rally team' back from Sweden in Stuttgart: Prince Fürstenberg, Ferry Porsche, Count von Berckheim, Count von Hardenberg, Prince zu Fürstenberg (from left to right).

31-3582

Fresh off the assembly line and already tackling a rally: this Porsche 356 Cabriolet was driven by 'Jocki' Prince zu Fürstenberg, and 'Tin' Count von Berckheim in June 1950 at the Rally to the Midnight Sun in Sweden.

# 92_ Liège–Rome–Liège, 1952

*Knockout in the fog*

Flashback to the early 1950s. Daring women and men in a dash across Europe. The challenge in road races such as the 'Grand Championnat d'Endurance Automobile Liège–Rome–Liège' was to cover incredible distances as quickly as possible. An extraordinary test for the crews and their cars.

From 13-18 August, 1952, this 'Marathon de la Route' took competitors over 5,168 kilometres through Belgium, Luxembourg, France, Italy and Germany, then back to Belgium. Twelve mountain passes were to be crossed in both directions. As the previous year's winners had had the effrontery to finish the marathon within the impossible time limits, the organisers decided to extend the route by 400 kilometres and increase the required average speed from 50 to 60 kph. Porsche driver Helmut Polensky later reported that the increase in average speed 'demanded driving almost all of the stages on a razor's edge [...] and at real racing speed on the mountain legs.' Porsche sent four lightweight 356 SL coupés with 1.5-litre engines to the start in Spa, equipped with '1 saw, 16 lightbulbs, 20 fuses, 2 pushrods with tappets, 2 front-wheel bearings, 2 spare wheels, 2 petrol pipes, 2 padlocks, 2 cleaning cloths.'

The line-up of competitors included all the big names: Ferrari, Lancia, Jaguar, Frazer Nash. Helmut Polensky and Walter Schlüter emerged as the fastest Porsche team in a 356 SL borrowed from the Belgian racing driver Gilberte Thirion. On the return journey through Italy, they fought a close duel at the front of the field with Umberto Maglioli in a Lancia. The Italian had to give up in the French Alps with mechanical problems. Polensky, now in the lead, delivered a knock-out blow to his rivals with a devilish drive across the foggy Galibier Pass. He was 12 seconds slower than the ideal time, while the second-placed Jaguar arrived 4:09 minutes after the ideal time. Polensky and Schlüter won, with five Porsches finishing in the top ten. On August 17, 1952, Porsche announced 'the fulfilment of a dream'. The young racing team had gained its first overall victory in one of the world's greatest road races.

— Helmut Polensky's and Walter Schlüter's 356 Gmünd Coupé at the 1952 Liège-Rome-Liège road race: '... driving almost all of the stages on a razor's edge.'

81
LIEGE ROME LIEGE

# 93__12 Hours of Sebring, 1960

*A nice vacation*

Officially, Porsche's first overall victory at the 12 Hours of Sebring in 1960 was not scored by the factory outfit. This was not possible, firstly because the regulations of the endurance classic did not allow works teams to compete. And secondly, the sponsor of the second world championship race of the year, which was held on March 26 on the notoriously bumpy concrete track in the middle of nowhere in Florida, was the giant US oil company Amoco.

And Porsche was tied to BP. Nevertheless, a bunch of fortunate coincidences and big-hearted acts of friendship made it possible for a team from Zuffenhausen to compete. Huschke von Hanstein, head of racing, made a spontaneous decision to take his vacation in the swampy solitude of central Florida. A group of mechanics thought this was a great idea and followed their boss, boarding a plane to the East Coast of the USA. The Swedish works driver, Joakim Bonnier, hit upon the idea, completely out of the blue, of entering two brand-new 718 RS60 Spyders borrowed from Zuffenhausen under his name. As Hanstein was a close friend of Bonnier, the racing baron agreed to manage the Swede's entry in the race in his free time. It goes without saying that all of the mechanics were also good friends of Bonnier. Of course they would pick up their screwdrivers for Joakim! Bonnier and Graham Hill drove one of the Porsches, Olivier Gendebien and Hans Herrmann the second.

At first, the 160 hp 1.6-litre 'pygmy Porsches', as American fans called the dashing little silver cars, were far behind the 4.6-litre Corvettes, the 3-litre Ferraris and the 2.9-litre Maseratis. But the heat and the mercilessly bumpy track took their toll. At the halfway stage, Hill and Bonnier had long dropped out with engine trouble, but Herrmann and Gendebien were running in third place. As the sun dropped below the horizon, the Swabian and the Belgian took the lead. A 718 RS60 from the American Brumos team was holding on to second place. And it stayed like that to the finish: a one-two victory for Porsche ahead of six Ferrari 250s. What would motor racing be without good friends on vacation?

__ The racing mechanic Eberhard Storz was one of a small group of Porsche technicians who just happened to be on the spot when this 718 RS60 drove to a first win in Sebring in 1960.

42

# 94_ Formula 2 at Monaco, 1959

*Porsche's first single-seater*

Porsche and monoposto racing weren't regarded a good match at Zuffenhausen. The difference between single-seaters and production sports cars seemed too great, and the race distances were too short for demonstrating reliability at high speeds.

But then in 1957, Formula 2 allowed sports cars like the Porsche 550 A Spyder to enter, which made the whole thing a lot more attractive to the German company. In 1958, the sports authorities drew up the rules to take effect in Formula 1 from 1961: 1.5-litre naturally aspirated engines, a minimum weight of 500 kilos. Now this was a perfect fit for Porsche, as the 1.5-litre Carrera engine looked promising at 160 hp, and 500 kilos was no problem for a specialist in lightweight construction. So Porsche gave it a go. Formula 2 was to be the door into Formula 1. Porsche entered the 718 RSK with mid-steering in 1958, and design work began on the 718/2 – a slightly modified open-wheel 718 – in 1959. Its slender shell of sheet aluminium clung to a steel space frame, and the synchronised six-speed gearbox of the 456-kilo single-seater was geared to a top speed of 250 kph.

On May 10, 1959, Count Wolfgang Berghe von Trips lined up on the grid in Monaco for the very first race of a monoposto, open-wheel Porsche. The aristocrat's Grand Prix in car number six ended on the first lap following a crash with Cliff Allison's Ferrari and Bruce Halford's Lotus.

Development work in Zuffenhausen went ahead at high revs. The 718/2 was given a longer wheelbase and more refined aerodynamics for the 1960 season. Curious, the superstar Stirling Moss was invited to test drive the Porsche – he was full of praise. Porsche let Moss have a car for the whole Formula 2 season. The Swede Joakim Bonnier drove for the works team, but it was Moss who gained the first win for the first Porsche formula racing car, on April 30, 1960, at the Aintree Motor Racing Circuit north of Liverpool. He went on to score more wins in a 718/2 that year, and Hans Herrmann also won once. Meanwhile, the development of a Formula 1 car had already begun in Zuffenhausen...

— Count Wolfgang Berghe von Trips driving Porsche's Formula 2 car for the first time on May 10, 1959, in Monaco. The 718/2 weighed a mere 456 kilograms and was designed to reach 250 kph.

The early days of Porsche's single-seaters. German Grand Prix at Berlin's AVUS, August 2, 1959. Von Trips in the No. 14 Porsche 718/2, Jean Behra in his Behra-Porsche.

# 95_Nürburgring 1000 km, 1967

*First home win, brief flourish*

In the second half of the 1960s, Porsche developed racing cars at a seemingly breathless speed and sent the 904, 906, 910, 907, 908, 908/02, 908/03 and 917 out to the circuits within a mere six years from 1964 to 1969. The aim was clear: the small sports car manufacturer was on the way from class wins to overall success and finally to a world championship. The engineers in Zuffenhausen kept finding ever-more creative ways of turning the Porsche philosophy of air-cooled engines and lightweight design into successful reality.

By 1966, Porsche had already won the famous Targa Florio five times and had made its mark in the USA thanks to Joakim Bonnier's 'vacation team' at Sebring in 1960 (our story 93). In 1967, Gerhard Mitter scored a second European Hillclimb Championship in succession. But there were gaps in the list of successes: Le Mans, Daytona and – high on Porsche's wishlist – a home win in the 1,000-kilometre race at the Nürburgring. Now the 910 represented a big step forward. For the first time, the tubes of the steel space frame served as oil pipes, and from May 1967, inner-vented disc brakes were fitted on the front axle. At 575 kilos, the 910 was lighter, more rigid and, thanks to a Formula 1-spec suspension with light 13-inch wheels (906: 16 inch), more agile and faster than its predecessor. The engine options remained the same with the 225 hp six-cylinder or the eight-cylinder Formula 1 engine, generating up to 270 hp and run as a 2- or 2.2-litre version depending on the torque required.

Paul Hawkins and Rolf Stommelen notched up the sixth overall win at the Targa Florio with the eight-cylinder 910. Three weeks later, on May 28, 1967, the big moment finally arrived: Udo Schütz from the tiny town of Selters and Joe Buzzetta from New York City won the 1,000-kilometre race on the Nürburgring Nordschleife in a works 910, two-tenths of a second ahead of their teammates Hawkins and Gerhard Koch. In fact, it was a banner day for Porsche, with the 910s locking out the first four places. But the golden days of the 910 were soon over, as a faster successor, the 907, took its place on the grid at Le Mans on June 10.

— The Porsche pits at the 1,000-kilometre race on the Nürburgring in 1967. Joe Buzzetta and Udo Schütz attained the long-awaited home win with the 910.

SHELL
41
ORSCHE
17
S-ZL 123

# 96_Inspection of the 917, 1969

*Racing car ready, parking available*

March 1969: the 917 super racer is set to debut and win races in a few weeks time. But right now all hell has broken loose at Porsche. FIA, as motorsport's governing body, has informed the race department: Contrary to standard practice, the FIA officials want to see 25 finished racing cars for the sports homologation, not just a few examples and parts. FIA added: 'As this is unusual, we will grant you an additional four weeks, until April 21.'

At this point, there were only two 917s ready in Zuffenhausen. The engineer Hermann Burst, an aerodynamics specialist, had joined Porsche racing on January 1. Burst was blessed with organisational talent and an extraordinary ability to get things done. Porsche tasked him the job of making the impossible possible. As Burst explained in 2019: 'I took on the coordination and, with the foreman Hubert Mimler, our workshop head Herbert Linge and the engine man Werner Enz, set up a three-shift system. 45 people worked in assembly, ten did the pre-assembly, and on top of that was the engine and transmission production.'

When dawn broke on April 21, everyone had bags under their eyes, but 25 917s were ready (more or less). Then a final obstacle emerged: they were to be presented on the management car park but this was occupied by the bosses' cars! Now Frau Hagn, Ferdinand Piëch's secretary, was called into action. With a round of phone calls, she emptied the area within an hour. Using a length of string, Burst marked the line on which the 917s were to stand in a row at a specified distance apart. Then the gentlemen from the sports authorities arrived. As Burst recalls: 'All of the 917s were ready to drive, even though they were not finished. A FIA man climbed into number 12, drove to the factory gate and had to turn in reverse gear. Number 12 even had sprung suspension, whereas other 917s were on water pipes because we didn't have enough springs!' All the same, the FIA were satisfied, Porsche was happy, and Burst had one more bit of organising to do: a party with long tables, benches and beer for everyone who had helped with the birth of the 917.

___ The big day: 25 Porsche 917s, lined up like pearls on a string on the management car park in Zuffenhausen. It would never have happened without Herr Burst and Frau Hagn.

D
4709

# 97_ Porsche 917 Leaves the USA, 1975

*Farewell with 1,230 hp*

There was too much to be done, and the engine in works driver Jo Siffert's 917/10 Spyder only held out for four laps. So no one felt in the mood for celebrating after the first test of Porsche's very first turbo racing engine on the short version of the Hockenheimring track on July 30, 1971. In retrospect, it seems a pity, as this day marked the start of Porsche's turbo era.

The rest of the year passed by with work on the drivability and robustness of the 4.5-litre, 12-cylinder motor, developing a sturdy four-speed gearbox and beefing up the brakes, which were under a lot of strain from 850 hp. For the premiere at the first event in the Can-Am series at Mosport Park, Canada, on June 11, 1972, the engine had grown to 5 litres. With his fastest qualifying lap, racing driver Mark Donohue planted the 917/10 entered by Porsche's partner Penske Racing on pole position for the race and finished second. After a testing accident forced Donohue to take a break, George Follmer took over the 917/10 and achieved the first win for a Porsche turbo engine on July 9 at Road Atlanta. By the time the penultimate event at Laguna Seca, California, came round, Follmer was already the overall winner and Porsche's first turbo champion.

Porsche raised the stakes for the 1973 season. The 917/30 weighed in at just 800 kilos. The 5.4-litre turbo engine generated over 1,000 hp. The first race on June 10 at Mosport Park with Mark Donohue at the wheel ended with seventh place following a shunting incident, the second race with second place, and then, from the third racing weekend at Watkins Glen on July 21–22 until the end of the year, Donohue was unbeaten. In an effort to revive the competition and the show on the circuits, the Can-Am series banned the Porsche. At its farewell to the USA on August 9, 1975, the 917/30 set a world record: Porsche fitted a five-litre V12 with intercoolers. The engine produced 1,230 hp at 8,300 revs, the exterior of the 917/30 had extremely low drag, and Mark Donohue drove extremely courageously. He turned three laps of the Trioval at Talladega, Alabama, in light rain at an average speed of 355.848 kph. A fitting conclusion to the story of the 917 Turbo-Spyder.

___ The 917/30 sported a very streamlined exterior for the world-record attempt at Talladega. Manfred Jantke, the head of press relations, glances into the cockpit of the 1,230 hp racing car.

ROCK BRAKE PRODUCTS
SERVING NASCAR GRAND NATION
RACING CIRCUIT THROUGHOUT
DieHard
GOODYEAR
6
CAM2
MOTOR OIL
GOODYEAR
CAM2
6
PORSCHE
EQUIPPED WITH
CHAMPION
SPARK PLUGS
NORTON

# 98_ Downforce vs Top Speed at Le Mans

*The end of a dogma*

Practice was underway for the 24 Hours of Le Mans in 1973. Ernst Fuhrmann, Porsche's CEO, visited his team in the pits and learned that his 911 Carrera RSRs had lost 12 kph on the long Mulsanne straight compared with the maximum speed during the April pretests. And top speed was regarded as the key to success at Le Mans. Fuhrmann was annoyed. Seriously annoyed. Lack of power was not the cause: at 320 hp, the three-litre naturally aspirated engine was in good fettle.

Fuhrmann asked Norbert Singer, a young engineer who had come to Le Mans with the works squad for the third time. Singer was a wizard in the wind tunnel, having given the 1,000 hp 917 huge wings for the Can-Am series in recent years, to great success. For Le Mans, Singer had shaped an impressive spoiler around the rear of the 911 and widened the rear-wheel housings to accommodate 14-inch tyres. Both measures were bad news for the top speed, but Singer swore that with the 'Mary Stuart collar', as the team called the spoiler, speed would be higher around the new Porsche Curve. The 911 would be more stable on the road and on the whole easier to drive. What's more, tyre wear would be less. Hence, over the whole distance, the car would be faster. Fuhrmann was sceptical and wanted to reduce the drag. Take off the windscreen wipers? Cut away the rain channel? The subject loomed over Singer like a thundercloud. He made sure to steer clear of the boss in the days building up to the race.

Before the start on Saturday, Fuhrmann, still angry, laid down his race strategy to the team: 'We'll go all out, like in qualifying.' Singer was very unhappy, the drivers anticipated an early end to their stint. In the race, Gijs van Lennep and Herbert Müller went full throttle. And Singer's prediction came true: easier to drive, gentler on the tyres, faster through the Porsche Curve. Behind three prototypes, described at the time as 'Formula 1with bodywork', the relatively tame production racer from Porsche finished a sensational fourth. The old dogma about top speed as the key to success at Le Mans was seriously shaken...

A works 911 Carrera RSR in Le Mans in 1973 sporting the 'Mary Stuart collar'. With this large spoiler, Porsche initiated the quest for downforce even on high-speed courses.

48
MARTINI RACING
46
MARTINI INTERNATIONAL CLUB
MARTINI
BOSCH
DUNLOP
TIRES
46
MARTINI RACING
Shell

# 99_ China's First Permanent Racetrack

*Premiere at Zhuhai*

Mopeds loaded with dozens of live chickens speed down the expressway, and people are going through their morning tai chi ritual in the hot, humid air at the shore of the Pearl Sea. There's a model of a MIG made out of butter in the hotel lobby, while the driveway outside is full of real Ferraris and Porsches, after all, this is a special economic zone. In the evenings, cages of raccoons and barrels of watersnakes stand in front of the restaurant: all meals are freshly prepared and washed down with 'Great Wall' wine, red or white. Locals and visitors eye each other up curiously. This is Zhuhai on the west coast of the Pearl River delta north of Macau in autumn 1996.

Less than a mile from the coast at the foot of wooded hills, thousands of workers are engaged in a final spurt, grafting day and night, because the first race on China's first permanent racetrack – Zhuhai International Motor Racing Circuit – is to take place on November 3, 1996. Only a few days remain before the start, and the pits, the grandstands and the hospitality facilities are still construction sites. However, on the Friday morning before the start of the first practice, everything is in place, perfect – and functioning. Unbelievable. This marks the third visit to Zhuhai for the BPR Global GT Series, the leading Gran Turismo championship. In the two previous years, the action took place in the city on the Zhuhai Street Circuit. A private team, Larbre Compétition, won China's first international motor race in 1994 with a 911 Turbo S LM GT (our story 32).

Now, it is time for the premiere of the Motor Racing Circuit. Twenty-eight cars line up for the start: Porsche, Ferrari, McLaren, Marcos. Even the Porsche works team has entered two 911 GT1s, as the company promotes GT sport. Two young drivers, Germany's Ralf Kelleners and the Frenchman Emmanuel Collard are given their first chance in a works car – and they grab it, with the best time in qualifying and a win in the four-hour race. Until 2011, GT championships returned to China's first permanent racetrack before the Formula 1 circuit in Shanghai became the People's Republic's great motor racing magnet.

Full house at Zhuhai. On November 3, 1996, China's first permanent racetrack was opened – with a win by a Porsche 911 GT1 96.

BPR
35
Marlboro
MICHELIN
BILSTEIN

Air-cooled or water-cooled, with or without a roof, turbo or four-wheel-drive. Regardless of its vintage, the 911 is Porsche's emotional heart. Pictured here is a lightweight Turbo S from 1992.

# AIR & WATER

Supercar Champion
IMSA

# 100_Generation 1: the First Porsche 911

*S presses ahead*

The first 911: unveiled in September 1963 at the IAA motor show in Frankfurt as the Porsche 901. Apart from the position of the air-cooled engine at the rear, the new model shows no trace of its predecessor, the 356. Ferdinand Piëch (whose thesis was on an F1 engine) and Hans Mezger (yes, the TAG-turbo Mezger) designed the six-cylinder engine. The test department – that's where Porsche's racing cars are made - has developed the chassis and suspension. Series production will begin – as the story is handed down – after only 13 prototypes, on September 14, 1964.

Six further versions of the first-generation model will follow until 1973. Porsche distinguishes them as the A to F models, starting with 1,991 cc and 130 hp and finishing in 1973 with the RS, as the crowning glory, offering 210 hp from 2.7 litres.

The precursor of the development, from the early days to the RS, was the 911 S, the story of which began in summer 1966 with an astounding 80 hp per litre. 160 hp was achieved thanks to forged metal-alloy pistons, sports camshafts and larger valves. There were anti-roll bars on both axles, Koni shock absorbers and, for the first time on a road-going Porsche, ventilated disc brakes all round. The 'windmill' wheels forged from metal alloy by Fuchs were classic features. From summer 1968, manifold injection yielded an additional 10 hp, and the wheelbase grew to 2,268 millimetres, which helped the handling. From September 1969, the 911 engines had a displacement of 2,195 cc, which translated to 180 hp for the 911 S. In 1971, the flat-six reached another peak in engine capacity with 2,341 cc and now 190 hp. Plenty good enough to accelerate the 1,075-kilo 911 S from standstill to 100 kph in seven seconds with a top speed of 230 kph.

This kind of power asked for special measures and the 911 S impressed with a further innovation: the first front spoiler worth its name on a sports car for the road. Porsche produced a total of 111,995 of the Ur-911. No wonder the 911 S, of which only 5,054 were manufactured, is a sought-after rarity today.

__ A wistful glance at the 911 S 2.0 – the 1967 model, which produced a sensational 80 hp per litre of engine displacement. It remains a mystery where the gentleman is going. Clearly not aboard the DC8.

THE FLYING DUTCHMAN
THOMAS ALVA EDISON

THOMAS ALVA EDISON
KLM

Version two of the wonderful PR shot featuring the 911 S 2.0. The name of the DC8 is somehow prophetic.

# 101_Generation 2: Porsche 911, G Series

*As you like it*

Porsche produced the second 911 generation for a longer period than any other. 198,496 sports cars in the G Series, as it was generally known, were made between 1973 and 1989. What they all have in common is the galvanised bodywork, front seats with automatic safety belts and integrated headrests, as well as concertina-style impact bumpers, which Style Porsche skilfully converted into a stylistic element under its head designer Anatole Lapine.

During those 17 years, the G Series evolved into a breathtakingly diverse number of variations. The flat-six engine grew from 2.7 to 3 litres and in 1983 to 3.2 litres with up to 250 hp. In 1974, in spite of the so-called energy crisis, Porsche took a bold step to launch the 911 Turbo, with a 3-litre displacement and 260 hp. In 1977, the output grew to 300 horsepower thanks to 3.3 litres of capacity and an intercooler. The turbo sprinted in 5.2 seconds from zero to 100 kph and reached its maximum speed at 260 kph. In contrast to exotic cars with similar performance data, the racer from Swabia did this reliably and in all weather (provided the driver's nerves were strong enough). The only other car to display comparable vigour was the Carrera RS 3.0, of which Porsche manufactured 110 cars – as a basis for motorsports.

Here's just a brief peek at the diversity of the G Series: After 20 years as a Coupé and Targa, the first 911 Cabriolet finally appeared on the road in 1983. The open-top 911 SC immediately proved to be extremely popular. A nod to the world of motorsport was the 1982 to 1989 small series of the slant-nose turbo model, with a design reminiscent of the world championship-winning 935. The diversity of the model family grew further in 1986–87 with the first Carrera Clubsport. By applying the art of omission – for example of back seats, anti-corrosion, radio, air-conditioning and electric windows – Porsche reduced the weight and boosted the enthusiasm of sporty drivers. Speaking of enthusiasm: Porsche took up a 1950s theme in 1989 with the 911 Carrera Speedster. It goes without saying that this last variation on the G Series is now a valuable classic car.

___ After two decades with (more or less) a roof, a truly open 911 finally arrived in 1983. The 911 SC Cabriolet produced 204 hp and could reach 235 kph.

6
4
4

___ The 911 Carrera 3.2 Cabriolet also came in the wide turbo-look. Here, the American version of the 1985 model.

# 102_Generation 3: Porsche 911, Type 964

*'We'll make a 4WD 911'*

The story of this revolution has a rather slippery start. Helmuth Bott, board member for research and development, and Peter Falk, head of testing, drove to the Monte Carlo Rally in 1981 in one of the first Audi Quattros to see what four-wheel drive was all about. On the tour, they had something of an Aha! moment: starting uphill on snow was possible with unprecedented grip. Falk recalled in his autobiography that: 'We were absolutely delighted with the traction and on the journey home decided that we should make a four-wheel-drive 911.'

The Porsche 953, the first Paris–Dakar 911 SC 4WD, and the 959 were milestones on the way to the first Nine-Eleven with four-wheel-drive to be built in large numbers. And it was the 4WD Carrera 4 that Porsche unveiled first in the summer of 1988. The centre differential distributed the power in a ratio of 31:69 to the front and the rear axle. If the ABS sensors registered slippage, the multi-disc clutch re-allocated torque. Porsche advertised the 964 as the world's fastest 4WD and as 85 per cent new, including the 3.6-litre boxer engine. The world's first series-production engine with a three-way catalytic converter produced 250 hp. The suspension system with metal-alloy control arms and coil springs instead of the traditional torsion bars was also a first for the Nine-Eleven. ABS now came as standard just like power steering and airbags (from 1991). At 80 kph, the retractable rear spoiler emerged automatically and disappeared discreetly at 10 kph. The 1,450-kilo 911 sprinted to 100 kph in 5.6 seconds and had a top speed of 260 kph.

To emphasise the endurance qualities of the new 911, in 1988 Porsche sent a Carrera 4 from Ushuaia, the southernmost town in the world, to Hammerfest, the northernmost, in three weeks. Six months after the debut of the 4WD, Porsche presented the 911 Carrera 2 with rear-wheel-drive to the public. By the time production ended in 1994, Zuffenhausen had made 74,008 third-generation 911s, including such coveted collector's items as the Carrera RS, the Turbo S and the Carrera 2 Speedster.

___ The lightweight 911 Turbo S was a powerful representative of the 964 generation. Only 86 were made. It weighed 1,290 kilos, put 381 hp on the rear axle, and sold out immediately at a price of 295,000 Deutschmarks.

— Something's brewing. Stripped to the bare minimum and with a dry weight of 1,220 kilos, the 911 Carrera RS 3.6 from 1991–92 could reach 100 kph in 5.3 seconds.

PORSCHE
S-EP 1470

# 103_Generation 4: Porsche 911, Type 993

*Finale furioso*

It's been a while since the Type 993 was made. What has survived the rocky road of history and stayed in the memory? It's obvious: this was the last air-cooled 911. Porsche unveiled the fourth-generation 911 in September 1993, just in time for the 30th anniversary of the sports car classic. Initially, its 3.6-litre, flat-six put out 272 hp. Later, the performance rose to 286, then 300 hp. The harmony of the six-cylinder motor and the new six-speed gearbox was a delight to behold, and for the first time in a 911, the heating worked really well. The new aluminium multi-link rear axle raised the possible cornering speeds and stability. No wonder: the former head of racing, Peter Falk, was responsible for developing it.

The 993 looked fantastic with its flatter front wings, curvy waist and integrated bumpers. Fast, beautiful, and unaggressive. Hats off to the designer Harm Lagaaij, under whose aegis the 911 Cabriolet, as well as the Targa with the smart glass roof and a wonderful Speedster (as a one-off for F.A. Porsche's 60th birthday), were also created. The 911 GT1 96 racing version was the first mid-engine 911 to compete at Le Mans in June 1996. Okay, to be honest only the front part was derived from the 993, while the rear end very much resembled that of the 962. On July 15 of the same year, Zuffenhausen celebrated the millionth Porsche, a police 911. In the intervening time, the new 911 Turbo had caused a stir at the Geneva motor show in March 1995: Its 3.6-litre, flat-six put out 408 hp.

With two small and light turbochargers instead of a single, heavier unit, the motor reacted instantly to the throttle pedal, and the thrust was mighty. 504 Newton-metres and permanent four-wheel-drive pushed the 911 Turbo from standstill to 100 kph in 4.5 seconds. Top speed: 290 kph. In the WLS version (factory tuning) and the 911 GT2, 450 hp were on offer.

Production of the Type 993 ended in July 1998 after 68,881 had been made. But the very last one was assembled by Porsche in 2018 from 6,500 original parts and auctioned as the 993 Turbo S 'Project Gold' for the Ferry Porsche Foundation. It fetched 2.7 million euros. A finale furioso.

___ The very last 993, a Turbo S reproduced from original parts by Porsche ten years after production stopped. It was auctioned as 'Project Gold' for the Ferry Porsche Foundation for 2.7 million euros.

# 104_Generation 5: Porsche 911, Type 996

*Watershed model*

Porsche presented the fifth generation of the 911 at the IAA motor show in Frankfurt in September 1997 under the motto 'Evolution 911'. Yet after three and a half decades of air-cooled flat-sixes, this was more of a revolution than an evolution: a water-cooled, four-valve, six-cylinder powered the Type 996! From a capacity of 3.6 litres it produced 300 hp at 6,800 revs. Thanks to the free-revving motor, a weight reduction of almost 50 kilos compared to its predecessor, and the beautifully geared six-speed 'box, the new 911 reached 100 kph in just 5.2 seconds.

A little-known fact: the water-cooled engine was originally intended to power the fourth-generation 911. At the time, however, the Type 989 four-seater project, which was ultimately abandoned, tied up a number of developers. Water cooling had to wait – and a lot of younger engineers were given the opportunity to work on the 996. With its new suspension, the wheelbase extended by 78 millimetres, and with a more spacious passenger compartment, the fifth-generation sports car icon offered more comfort than its predecessor. Until production ceased as scheduled in 2005, Porsche produced the 996 in many variations – from the glass-roof Targa to the GT2 with 482 hp.

As a pure driving machine, the new 911 GT3 upheld the tradition of race-worthy, road-approved Porsche sports cars. Its development was the work of rallying legend Walter Röhrl and racing engineer Roland Kussmaul. With the crankshaft taken from the GT1, titanium connecting rods, racing pistons and dry-sump lubrication with a separate oil tank, the engine generated power equal to 360 full-bred horses. The bodywork based on the Carrera 4 sported side sills, a rear wing and a special front spoiler. Kussmaul and Röhrl tuned the adjustable suspension to knife-edge precision. For those who wished to travel at high speed with a little more comfort, Porsche offered air-conditioning or a radio at no extra cost. A rugged Clubsport version was equipped with a roll-over bar. At 179,500 Deutschmarks, the GT3 became a best-seller. Of the 175,262 996 produced up to 2005, 5,139 were GT3s. New versions across all subsequent 911 generations, dubbed GT3 R, RS and RSR, compete on racetracks to this day.

— 1,350 kilos, zero to 100 kph in 4.8 seconds, 302 kph top speed: the first-ever 911 GT3 was realised by the racing engineer Roland Kussmaul and the rally idol Walter Röhrl.

GT3
S-PR 494

# 105_Generation 6: Porsche 911, Type 997

*Don't overdo it!*

In July 2004, the curtain rose on the sixth-generation: the Type 997. For his last 911, head designer Harm Lagaaij reverted to the stylistic vocabulary of the 993, which had been his first. There were the round headlights, the integrated bumpers and the noticeable waist, emphasised on the 997 by a rear end that was 44 millimetres wider.

As we would have rightly expected, Porsche again set new benchmarks for driving performance and technical innovations. The 997 was, of course, more powerful than its 996 predecessor. The entry level was now 3.5 litres of displacement and 325 hp for the Carrera, while the Carrera S boasted 3.8 litres and 355 hp. The turbo model, available from 2006, turned heads with 480 hp and 620 Newton-metres – which set in earlier than before, as guide blades forced gas to flow at high speed onto the turbine wheels of the two turbos even at lower engine revs. The company named its innovation for petrol engines 'Variable Turbine Geometry', or VTG for short. The sprint to 100 kph was over after just 3.7 seconds.

In 2008, it was time for the next world premiere: the direct fuel injection that had been tested intensely on racetracks in the RS Spyder gave the entire range a boost in performance combined with more economical fuel consumption. From 2008, Porsche offered another development carried over from motorsport: the Porsche dual-clutch gearbox PDK: two-part gearboxes, each with its own clutch, make fully automatic gearshifts possible without interrupting the thrust. Simply put: rocket acceleration.

Some two years before the production of the 997 ended, Porsche set an exclamation mark in 2010 unveiling the 911 GT2 RS. 620 turbo hp from a 3.6-litre engine for a weight of 1,370 kilos (as light as the 993 had been), coupled with the very finest that Porsche could provide in terms of aerodynamics and suspension resulted in a record lap on the Nordschleife of the Nürburgring (7:18 min.). The GT2 RS was the first 911 to dash to 200 kph in under ten seconds: 9.8. Porsche capped the top speed to 330 kph. After all, Swabians prefer not to overdo it.

___ A 911 GT2 RS, 2011 model year: 620 horsepower for 1,370 kilograms. After producing 213,004 examples of the 997, Porsche set this exclamation mark at the end of the production.

GT2RS

# 106_Generation 7: Porsche 911, Type 991

*Records, records*

The autumn of 2011 heralds the launch of the seventh-generation 911. The track of the front axle has grown by almost five centimetres, and the new Nine-Eleven is seven millimetres lower than the previous model. Shorter overhangs with a ten-centimetre-longer wheelbase amplify the impression of power. The head of design, Michael Mauer, lent the first 911 created under his aegis the proportions and lines that typify this iconic sports car and added a few special delicacies like the wing mirrors or the headlights that evoke memories of the 718 racers from the 1960s.

A lot of ground-breaking work went into the Type 991, such as a completely new suspension. For the now more rigid bodyshell, the engineers saved up to 45 kilos with an aluminium-steel design. The new 911 was fitted with the world's first manually shifted seven-speed gearbox (PDK if desired). From spring 2012, the cabriolet version was available. Needless to say, it came with a Porsche invention: thanks to magnesium elements, the roof was almost as rigid as that of the Coupé. The GT3, launched in 2013 with 475 hp, sprinted from zero to 100 kph in 3.5 seconds, was capable of 315 kph and featured active rear-wheel steering. The Targa hit the showrooms in May 2014 – in the style of the first generation Targas: a dark roof, B-column bar of brushed steel, and a glass rear window. The roof opened and closed at the push of a button with a mechanism that only Weissach could have invented.

There was a drumroll at Porsche in 2015: from now on, all 911s, with the exception of the GT3, GT3 RS and specials like the Speedster, were to be turbos. To be more precise, twin-turbos. Starting with 370 hp from 3 litres in the Carrera, 420 hp in the Carrera S and 450 for the GTS, meant that even the entry-level 911 accelerated to 100 kph in less than 4 seconds. At the top of the range, the GT2 RS, producing 700 hp and shod with road-legal tyres, rocketed to a new record of 6:47 minutes on the Nordschleife. The millionth 911 rolled off the assembly line in Zuffenhausen on May 11, 2017. And on October 31, 2018, Porsche ceased production of the 991 after another record: 233,540 units made it the most-produced 911 model.

___ The 2019 Speedster was the last 991. 1,948 were produced, with a 510 hp naturally aspirated engine, six-speed manual gearbox and a manually operated top. Some solace in an era of smooth electronics.

LB CW 4002
48
48
PORSCHE
S VK 1948

# 107_Generation 8: Porsche 911, Type 992

*A clever beast*

On November 28, 2018, Porsche announced the 911 Type 992 in Los Angeles and opened the eighth chapter of the 911 story. The main topics of conversation were about electronics, communications and connectivity. But it's easy to recognise typical 911 features: the dashboard with five round gauges in a classical arrangement, with the large rev counter in the middle. Okay, the needle of the rev counter is the only mechanical thing here, everything else is digital.

The 10.9-inch 'centre screen' serves as the command centre for a long list of electronic aids. Porsche Communication Management, online at all times, navigates the 911 around congested traffic with the help of swarm data. The Wet Mode represents a worldwide first: when acoustic sensors in the front wheel housings detect moisture, the system suggests that the driver activates this mode. When activated, Porsche Stability Management, traction management and optional torque-vectoring leap into action. The electronics also ensure a silky-soft throttle response and raises the rear spoiler. For even more safety in nasty weather or poor light conditions, there's a warning and braking assistant on board. Plus, a thermal imaging camera recognises obstacles long before they appear in the beam of the headlights. Numerous apps assist in 'neutralising the individual carbon footprint', quoting the words of the press release. Or in finding your ideal personal line on 200 racetracks.

This is all well and good – but what is it like to drive the new Nine-Eleven? The S, with 450 turbo hp from a 3-litre engine, takes 3.6 seconds from a standing start to 100 kph and reaches its limit at 306 kph. Porsche fine-tuned the new generation of engines with Otto particle filters, new chargers, intercoolers, smart wastegates and piezo injection valves. Even overindulged professional testers found that the car has more punch from low revs and seemingly endless reserves up to top speed. Turn-in was beautiful, the cornering almost like on rails, and the brakes made their eyes pop out. To make it short: the philosophy of the 911 lives on in generation number eight.

Porsche presented the 911 Turbo S – the new vanguard – in March 2020. The 3.8-litre, flat-six biturbo generates 650 hp. After 2.7 very enjoyable seconds from standstill, the Turbo S travels at 100 kph.

___ The 2019 Porsche 911 Carrera 4S 3.0. Now in its eighth generation, the Nine-Eleven retains all the classic lines and proportions.

Porsche adds high-performance fully electric sports cars to the portfolio. Here, CEO Oliver Blume (left) and head of design Michael Mauer present the Taycan Cross Turismo to the media.

# WATTS & PUNCH

More space
Larger luggage compartment
PORSCHE
PORSCHE
Mission e

# 108_Electric Pioneer

*Magical energy*

'Now the wheel has come full circle back to my grandfather,' said Wolfgang Porsche, chairman of the supervisory board at a press conference about Porsche's commitment to electric vehicles in May 2018. Wolfgang Porsche's grandfather: the career that Ferdinand Porsche's father, Anton, had envisaged for his son was to become a plumber in the family business. But at the end of the 19th century, Ferdinand was fascinated by future opportunities: electric power, energy with incalculable potential. And automobiles, which meant mobility with a freedom never known before at speeds that could barely be imagined.

Ferdinand Porsche, born in September 1875, first supplied the family home in Maffersdorf in northern Bohemia with electric lighting and an electric doorbell in 1893 – a slice of the future for the house at number 38 Hauptstrasse. In the following years, Porsche combined the automobile and electric power in his design work. The Egger-Lohner C.2 Phaeton of 1898 was powered by Porsche's Octagon-Elektro engine. Two years later, the young visionary had transferred his engines into the front-wheel hubs of the Egger-Lohner Electromobile, in order to avoid complicated power transmission. His Semper Vivus, the first functional hybrid car, took to the roads in 1900. In that same year, Porsche installed four of his wheel-hub motors producing a total of 56 hp in an electric racing car for a British importer: the first four-wheel-drive passenger car. In 1902, Porsche drove from Vienna to his hometown – 400 kilometres on country roads – in the Lohner-Porsche Mixte, the series-production version of the Semper Vivus.

These were visionary vehicles, several decades ahead of their time. Everyday use was hindered by batteries that were much too heavy, recharging them proved virtually impossible and the cost of the e-vehicles was simply prohibitive. For the first hundred years, combustion engines won the race for progress. Now, however, the wheel has come full circle...

___ Ferdinand Porsche at the wheel of his Lohner Porsche electric racing car, with which he set a record in September 1900: 10 kilometres including 400 metres uphill in just under 15 minutes.

# 109_Mission E

*Simply electrifying*

It is spring 2020, and the atmosphere – as well as the buzzword – at Porsche is electric. The Taycan is on sale, and the factory in Stuttgart is planning on producing about 20,000 examples of this whisperingly quiet sports car every year. Photos taken in California have just showcased the new Taycan Cross Turismo – a high-class 'shooting brake' based on the latest Porsche. It was given the go-ahead in autumn 2018. The next generation of the best-selling Macan will also be electric, with production due to start in 2021. Six out of ten customers who buy the large Panamera opt for the plug-in hybrid version. Before the Covid-19 crisis, the forecast from Stuttgart-Zuffenhausen was that every second Porsche could be an electric vehicle as early as 2025.

Porsche has certainly put a lot of weight and money behind an electric future. About 2,000 new jobs have been created in Zuffenhausen alone to produce the Taycan. Porsche has invested a billion euros at the main plant, and by 2022 the figure will be six billion euros company-wide.

The concentrated shift to electric has also created an interesting situation in terms of the personnel structure. More than half of the new engineers have a background in IT or electronics. A great deal of energy is being expended in Weissach, it has been reported, to find ways of electrifying not just the Taycan Gran Turismo but also Porsche's nimble and light sports models such as the 718 Boxster and the 718 Cayman. Smaller and lighter batteries will be necessary to turn this intention into reality. Even the optimists in the field do not expect a breakthrough in this regard until the second half of this decade. It will take longer, perhaps much longer, until the first fully electric 911 makes its appearance. Insiders speculate that the 'porschest' of all Porsches, a monument to a long and fascinating era, will be powered by combustion engines for at least one more decade.

The Taycan Cross Turismo on a mountain road in California. You really can't call this elegant sports car a hatchback. The press calls it a 'shooting brake'.

PORSCHE
Mission e

# 110_Porsche 99X Electric

*High voltage racing*

PIP: Porsche Intelligent Performance. This was the motto in 2010 when Porsche sent the 911 GT3 R Hybrid to the racetracks. Since then, Porsche has explored the capabilities of electric power with ever-more urgency, most recently with the three-time Le Mans winner, the 919 Hybrid.

On August 29, 2019, the company unveiled its latest coup, the 99X Electric, a single-seater for the Formula E championship in 2019–20. This series, the first championship for all-electric racing cars, has been held on city circuits all around the world since 2014. In 2019–20, twelve teams from ten manufacturers entered 24 racing cars. Here again, motor racing serves to accelerate developments and to provide a training camp for engineers. The battery, chassis, aerodynamics, front axle and tyres are identical for all competitors. But the brains of the development and racing departments are given free rein to work on the electric motor, converter, brake-by-wire system, gearing, differential, drive shafts, cooling system, control devices and rear axle. Depending on whether the driver selects qualifying, racing or attack mode, the e-motor produces up to 250 kW (equivalent to 340 hp). The 99X Electric accelerates from zero to 100 kph in less than three seconds, with a top speed of around 280 kph.

The battle in qualifying for grid spots is brief and explosive: each driver has a maximum of six minutes to turn their fastest lap. The ePrix – i.e. the race – lasts 45 minutes plus one lap. The racing weekend is also short and sweet: functional tests on Friday, practice, qualifying and the race on Saturday. In this way, neither the patience of city residents nor the manufacturers' budgets are overtaxed. The same purpose is served by limiting the size of teams to 20 people at the circuits and the number of test days to 15 per year. The automobile manufacturers and the World Motorsport Council are putting their faith in the future of Formula E, which gained world championship status for the 2020–21 season.

— The Porsche 99X Electric for the 2019–20 season. The regulations prescribe covered wheels and a small tail-wing. As for the design: it's somewhat reminiscent of the Batmobile.

ANSYS
TAGHeuer
vodafone
vodafone
PORSCHE
TAGHeuer
ANSYS
TAGHeuer
ANSYS
Mobil
TAGHeuer
TAGHeuer

# 111_Porsche Taycan

*Racing to the future*

Porsche: the name, the design, the performance, the know-how and the passion to develop a unique sports car. The results are spectacular. A pre-production Taycan lapping the Nordschleife of the Nürburgring in record time, for example – 7:42 minutes of truth on the topic of handling and power. Or from zero to 200 kph in less than 10 seconds – thrust that 'the average person has never experienced,' as Walter Röhrl puts it.

Or the stories from testing. Porsche developers have always had brilliant ideas for putting their cars through hell. For example, driving the 911 in reverse gear for one kilometre after another at high revs. 1,000 engineers, technicians and test drivers have put the pre-series Taycan through its paces. With acceleration trials, for instance: 26 times from zero to 200, flat-tack, one sprint immediately after the other, no break. Six million test kilometres on roads in 30 countries, plus ten million kilometres per simulation.

The philosophy by which the racing cars for Le Mans were made right from the beginning lives on in the Taycan: the technology must be small, light and efficient. The Taycan is the first series-produced car with a system voltage of 800 volts. The power train operates at double the voltage of conventional electric vehicles, which means that the cables are only half as thick and heavy, losses in transmission are lower, and less space is required.

Or consider the copper wires for the stator winding of the two electric motors: they are not round but rectangular, and can therefore be more densely packed in 'hairpin winding'. This increases performance and torque for the same volume and is helpful for cooling. The active aerodynamics reduces the drag coefficient to as little as 0.22 – an outstanding result. The centre of gravity of the car is two centimetres lower than that of the 911 – this, too, makes the developers proud. It is as if the Taycan were ready to catapult off the grid at the start of a race tomorrow. E-mobility, Porsche-style.

___ The Taycan in temperatures below zero somewhere in the Arctic Circle. Deep-frozen trips and stop-and-go tests in Death Valley are all part of the development programme.

S GO 299E

**I would like to thank the following people:**
Achim Stejskal, director of the Porsche Museum in Stuttgart-Zuffenhausen, for always keeping the door to his museum open for me. Frank Jung, head of the company archive, made original documents and photos available without any frustrating red tape and was extremely helpful in assisting my work, with the support of Alexander von den Benken, Tilman Leitz, Sarah Pelters and Alexander Redmer. I would like to thank the archivist Jens Torner for his great and untiring help. My sincere thanks as well to Timo Bernhard, Astrid Böttinger, Hermann Burst, Peter Falk, Owen Hayes, Roland Heiler, Roland Kussmaul, Tobias Mauler, Allan McNish, Stephen Mummery, Norbert Singer, Herbert Linge, Valentin Schäffer, Alwin Springer and Christian Weiss.
All of them were very generous in sharing their time and knowledge with me.

For more than three decades, **Wilfried Müller** has been writing about cars, about people who make cars, and about daredevils who drive them. Born in Cologne, he travelled around the world for many years as a motorsports reporter, later wrote numerous books and discovered his passion for Porsche, a theme that occupies him to this day. Wilfried Müller lives in New Zealand with his wife and two children.

**Bibliographical information of the Deutsche Nationalbibliothek**
The Deutsche Nationalbibliothek lists this publication in the Deutsche Nationalbibliografie; detailed bibliographical data are available on the internet at http://dnb.d-nb.de.


Layout: Jörg Weusthoff, Weusthoff Noël, Hamburg
based on a conception by Lübbeke | Naumann | Thoben
Printing and binding: Optimal Media, Röbel/Müritz
English translation: John Sykes, Cologne; Wilfried and Kaye Müller, New Zealand

Printed in Germany 2020
ISBN 978-3-7408-0904-1
First edition

For the latest information about emons, subscribe to our regular newsletter at www.emons-verlag.de

FSC www.fsc.org MIX Paper from responsible sources FSC® C108521